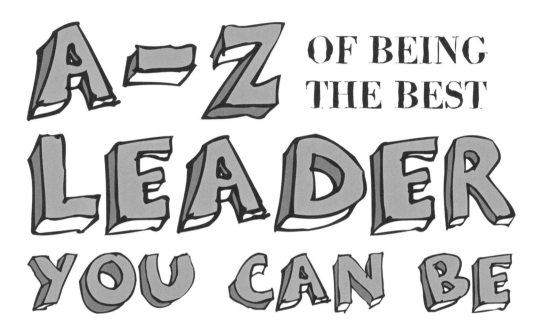

A-Z OF BEING THE BEST LEADER YOU CAN BE

Leading Through the Alphabet

— Yvonne Bleam —
— Illustrated by Kat Stahl —

Jessica Kingsley *Publishers*
London and Philadelphia

First published in 2016
by Jessica Kingsley Publishers
73 Collier Street
London N1 9BE, UK
and
400 Market Street, Suite 400
Philadelphia, PA 19106, USA

www.jkp.com

Library of Congress Cataloging in Publication Data
A CIP catalog record for this book is available from the Library of Congress

British Library Cataloguing in Publication Data
A CIP catalogue record for this book is available from the British Library

ISBN 978 1 78592 708 9
eISBN 978 1 78450 272 0

Printed and bound in China

ABOUT THE AUTHOR

Yvonne Bleam has a Doctorate of Strategic Leadership from Regent University. She has an MBA and BA in Behavioral Neuroscience from Lehigh University, works full-time for Novartis Oncology, and is a Professor of Executive Skills Leadership in the MBA Program at DeSales University. She lives in Allentown, Pennsylvania with her husband, Brian, and two children, Hunter and Brooke. She has been involved in various leadership roles within her church, community, and school, and recognizes the importance of leadership at every level. Using both her background in leadership, and her children as her inspiration, she developed the ever-important concepts in this book.

ACKNOWLEDGMENTS

This book was written for my children, Hunter and Brooke, who continually amaze me with their creativity, good moral choices, and displays of leadership!

For my loving husband, Brian, and the rest of my extended family – thank you for your encouragement, support, and patience. I could not have done it without you.

For children everywhere – you are not too young to be the kind of leader that can make a lasting difference in the world!

INTRODUCTION

The purpose of this book is to encourage and promote positive leadership behavior at an early age. Being a leader means having influence over other people. By integrating leadership concepts with simple, age-appropriate stories, children can learn to make good choices, be able to respond appropriately to others, and consequently, influence others to do the same. The foundation for this book is my belief that every child, regardless of his or her background or skillset, has the potential to be a leader. In fact, most of the concepts in this book are not skill-based, but are centered on positive behavior, making good choices, and interacting admirably with other people. Because of this behavioral-based approach, it is never too early to begin teaching the basic concepts and leadership lessons in this book. You can provide children with the tools that they need to make a lasting difference in the world, and promote behavior that will encourage success in life.

Each chapter is based on one letter of the alphabet and is organized as follows:

1. Name of the character and leadership concept.

2. A quote that is relevant to the leadership concept being discussed.

3. A brief, simple definition of the leadership concept.

4. A more in-depth description of what the leadership concept means for the child.

5. A short story or vignette demonstrating what it may look like to carry out that leadership concept.

6. Five discussion questions.

7. A leadership learning activity.

To reinforce the learning, there are four additional summary leadership learning activities at the end of the book.

This book can be used in a variety of settings: school or home-based classrooms, after-school programs, and community- or faith-based programs. It can easily be integrated into current leadership education or academic curriculum. The time commitment for group discussion could be as little as 10 minutes or as much as 30 minutes per chapter. For younger children (kindergarten through second grade), I recommend this solely as group discussion around each chapter's leadership trait. Older children (third through fifth grade) may benefit from independent work followed up with group discussion. Regardless of how this book is used, it is my hope and belief that children will develop attitudes of respect for self and others, and understand that they each can demonstrate these concepts and be a leader at any age.

CONTENTS

ALEX
THE ACCEPTING LEADER

> "I believe the sign of maturity is accepting others for who they are."

UNKNOWN AUTHOR

DEFINITION

Accepting Leader – You are open and tolerant, and accept others for who they are.

WHAT IT MEANS FOR YOU

When you are an accepting leader, you show others that you care and do not judge them because of their differences. By accepting others, you show that each person is important and their contribution is valuable. Being accepting of others does not mean that you will always agree with them but that you accept their differences and respect them as people.

ALEX
THE ACCEPTING LEADER

It was the fourth week of school and as Alex rode the bus on his way there, he sighed in relief because he had finally figured out his weekly routine. Alex began to mentally check off what special activities he had each day of the week. He thought about each day. "Monday is computer day. Tuesday is music. I have to remember my recorder next week or Mrs. Eldred will give me a disciplinary slip if I forget again," he shuddered as he thought about it. She could be pretty tough. He continued thinking about his schedule. "Wednesday is library. I cannot wait to borrow the newest *Diary of a Wimpy Kid* book." He thought about his mom and smiled because she roared with laughter every night when they read books from the series together. Sometimes she laughed so loud that she woke up his baby sister.

He then thought about Thursday being art class. "I'm a pretty good artist," Alex said to himself. "Not as good as Ellen Buggy but not bad either." "Why did she always have to bring up his self-portrait from first grade?" he wondered. So what if he looked like a spiky-haired hedgehog. Come to think of it…the drawing did look a lot like him.

He actually did resemble a spiky-haired hedgehog most of first grade. Alex thought about how much he hated getting his hair cut that year and how he tried to spike his uncontrollable hair with his dad's hair gel. "Oh well…live and learn," he thought. A smile spread across his face as he thought about Friday being gym day. "The best day of the week!" he told himself. Gym was something he always felt good about. He knew he was a good athlete and the gym teacher really liked him.

So when Friday came, Alex was ready for action. He knew that they would be playing dodge ball in gym and he and his three closest friends had figured out Mr. Slap's method of picking teams. Alex told Drew, Matt, and Mason, "Line up so that there are three kids between each of us." Sure enough, Mr. Slap counted off by fours and they ended up on a team together. The fifth person on their team was the new kid in school, Leo Rambino. Leo had just moved into Alex's third grade class at Brandt Elementary School two days ago. Alex had not really spoken to him yet but heard from his friends that Leo didn't play any sports and that he seemed a little strange.

Alex's three friends started complaining to him about Leo. "We'll never win now!" they whined to Alex. "We need to come up with a plan," said Drew. They had to wait until the second game to play, so while waiting, the four boys decided who would be their first target on the other team. They also decided to put Leo right in the front so he would get out first. Leo tried to hear what they were saying but just stepped back when he realized that they weren't going to include him in their plan. Alex felt bad for Leo but wanted so badly to win that he ignored him too.

The boys' plan worked. They picked off each person on the other team and Leo was the only one on their team to get out. They were so proud of themselves. The boys gave each other high fives on the way back to class. Leo trailed behind them. Alex turned around and saw the look of disappointment on Leo's face. He felt guilty about how he and his friends had behaved. He thought to himself, "Maybe winning isn't worth hurting someone else."

That afternoon, as they ran out to the playground for recess, Drew, Matt, and Mason grabbed Alex and said, "Let's see if we can play dodge ball again!"

Alex told them, "Go ahead. I have to do something else first." They rolled their eyes at him and ran ahead.

Alex waited for Leo to catch up to him. "Hey, I'm sorry about gym class," Alex said.

"That's alright. I'm not very good at sports," said Leo.

"What do you like to do?" asked Alex.

Leo hesitated. "Well, I really like to draw. I'm working on a comic strip right now. Do you want to see it?"

"You bet I do!" exclaimed Alex. They spent the whole recess looking at Leo's drawings and his latest comic strip. Alex thought Leo's drawings were great and he realized that Leo was a really funny kid. "Who knows, maybe he can teach me how to draw so I can finally beat Ellen Buggy!" he thought to himself.

Alex's friends wondered what happened to him during recess. When they got back to class, Alex told them, "You need to see some of Leo's comic strips. He's really funny." They hesitated, but when they took a look at some of Leo's work, they realized Alex was right and Leo was a cool, funny kid.

Alex thought to himself, "Leo may not be a good athlete, but I'm sure glad that I took the time to get to know him." Because of Alex, Leo was accepted by the other kids, and they were all glad to have a new, really funny friend!

LET'S DISCUSS

1. What does it mean to be an accepting leader?

2. What did Alex do to show that he was an accepting leader?

3. How do you think Leo felt because Alex accepted him for who he was?

4. What may have happened if Alex did not make the effort to accept Leo?

5. In what ways can you be an accepting leader to others?

LEADERSHIP LEARNING ACTIVITY

Use the following empty comic strip boxes to draw three scenes from the story about Alex the Accepting Leader. Make the scenes as simple or as creative as you want.

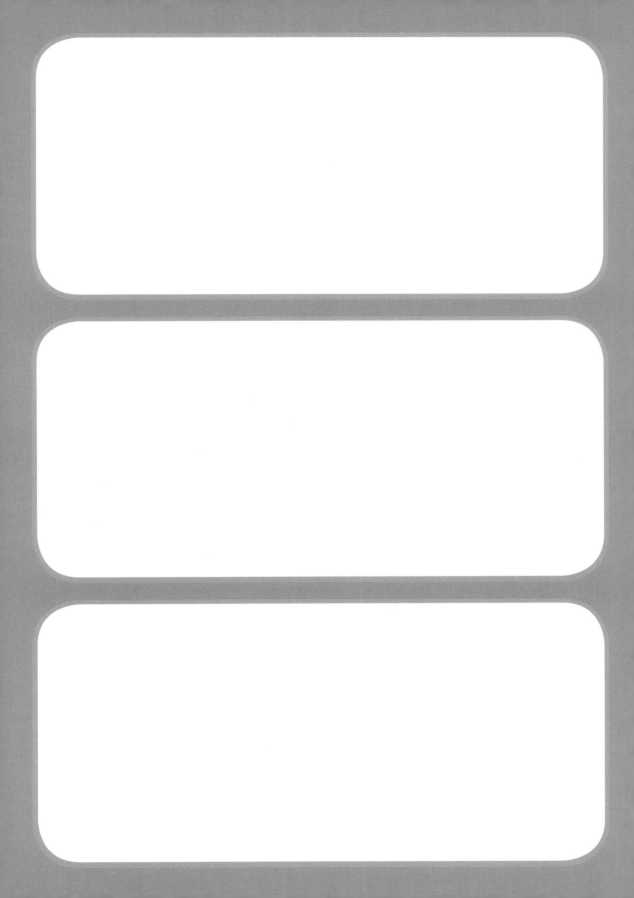

BROOKE
THE BRAVE LEADER

"We must dare to be great;
and we must realize that
greatness is the fruit of toil and
sacrifice and high courage."

TEDDY ROOSEVELT

DEFINITION

Brave Leader – You are not afraid to make a personal sacrifice for others.

WHAT IT MEANS FOR YOU

When you are a brave leader, you demonstrate courage and inspire others to be courageous too. You are willing to take risks, especially to help others. When you are a brave leader, you may choose to go through uncomfortable situations for the benefit of others.

BROOKE
THE BRAVE LEADER

Brooke paused as she walked into the girls' bathroom. Sure enough, Karla Klinger was in there and looked like she was causing trouble again. She sneered at Brooke and brushed against her shoulder as she walked out. Brooke wondered to herself, "What is Karla up to this time?" It didn't take her long to realize what Karla was sneering about. There was new graffiti on the back of the stall door. Brooke read the message, "Maggie Kelly smells like a cow!" She then recalled the argument between Karla and Maggie earlier that day. Brooke thought about it. "Well it wasn't so much an argument as it was Maggie not giving Karla her snack money as usual." Brooke guessed that was enough of a reason to cause Karla to write that mean message. "Why does she always bully people?" Brooke wondered. She didn't know if she should get involved, and if she did, what exactly she should do.

As Brooke walked back to class, she thought about her different options. 1. She could act like nothing happened and go about her day. 2. She could tell some of her other friends what she saw and hope that one of them would do something about it. 3. She could tell the teacher about the graffiti message and that she saw Karla leaving the bathroom looking suspicious. She worried to herself, "What if Ms. Snapper says that doesn't prove anything? Worse yet, what if Karla comes after me next?"

She didn't have time to think any more about it once she got back to the classroom. Ms. Snapper was handing out the spelling tests. She made it back just in time. Her mouth turned up at the corner and she smiled to herself as Ms. Snapper handed her the test paper. Ms. Snapper really did look like a wise old snapping turtle with her rounded back, short arms, and glasses dangling at the tip of her pointy nose. "She might look like a turtle but she is also one of the nicest teachers I have ever had," thought Brooke.

On the way to lunch, Brooke was distracted, thinking about what she had seen in the bathroom. She had nearly made up her mind to not tell anyone about it and act like it never happened when she saw Karla bullying Rosa. Rosa Montez was the smallest and one of the shyest girls in the class. She also happened to have a stuttering problem. It got worse when she became nervous and Karla knew it. She had cut in front of Rosa in the lunch line and was trying to get Rosa to speak up and embarrass herself with her stuttering. "What's wrong, Rosa? Sounds like you have a jackhammer in your throat?" laughed Karla.

That's it! "I don't care if she does come after me next!" Brooke thought bravely. She was not going to quietly sit back and allow Karla to bully anyone else. Someone had to put a stop to it. "Why not me?" Brooke decisively asked herself. She trembled a little but walked right up to Karla and said, "Karla, leave Rosa alone! I also know what you did in the bathroom! I'm going to go talk to Ms. Snapper and Mrs. Fowler, the principal, about it right now!"

Karla sneered at her and said, "You wouldn't dare, you little worm!"

Brooke turned around and told the lunch monitor she had to go to the principal's office immediately. She barely made it to the office because her legs felt like rubber bands, they were shaking so badly. She sat down with Mrs. Fowler and Ms. Snapper and shared what she had seen in the bathroom and what she just saw Karla doing to Rosa.

From that point forward, Karla no longer got away with bullying. Mrs. Fowler and Ms. Snapper made sure of it. Karla had to apologize to

Rosa and Maggie in front of the whole class, and during detention, she had to scrub the graffiti off all the bathroom stalls. Because of Brooke being a brave leader, the other kids were also not as afraid to stand up to Karla and the other bullies.

LET'S DISCUSS

1. What does it mean to be a brave leader?
2. Why is it sometimes hard to be a brave leader?
3. How do you think Rosa and Maggie felt because of Brooke standing up for them?
4. What may have happened if Brooke didn't stand up to Karla?
5. In what ways can you be a brave leader?

LEADERSHIP LEARNING ACTIVITY

What does being brave look like to you? Is it a superhero? Is it doing something that is hard, like meeting new people or playing a new sport or a new instrument? Is it someone like Brooke, who stands up to a bully? Draw a picture of yourself being brave.

CHLOE
THE CULTURALLY SENSITIVE LEADER

"Freethinkers are those who
are willing to use their minds
without prejudice and without
fearing to understand things that
clash with their own customs,
privileges, or beliefs."

LEO TOLSTOY

DEFINITION

Culturally Sensitive Leader – You appreciate the cultural differences in others.

WHAT IT MEANS FOR YOU

When you are a culturally sensitive leader, you demonstrate a greater awareness, sensitivity, and positive appreciation of others' cultural, religious, and social beliefs. You respect other people regardless of those differences. You also take time to appreciate and understand why others may have different feelings, wishes, rights, or traditions.

CHLOE
THE CULTURALLY SENSITIVE LEADER

Chloe and Becca sat next to Ranju at lunch. "What in the world is Ranju eating?" Chloe wondered. Her mom never made anything that remotely looked like the stuff Ranju brought to school every day. The most unusual meal her mom ever made was green eggs and ham to celebrate Dr. Seuss week. Her dad didn't consider that dinner though because it didn't include both a meat and a potato. Chloe didn't mind that Ranju ate different things than her but she wondered why it always smelled so strange. Chloe knew Becca and some of her other friends would say something about it again after lunch.

As they were walking back to class, sure enough Becca exclaimed, "Ranju – why do you eat such strange, stinky food? Why does your mom always pack you stuff like that? You should ask her to pack you a Luncheable like my mom gives me!" Ranju looked a little embarrassed.

Chloe elbowed Becca and said to Ranju, "Please don't start eating like Becca! She eats the same exact Luncheable for breakfast, lunch, and most dinners! Because of her, they should be called 'Everymealable!'" Ranju relaxed a little and laughed with Chloe and Becca. The girls then chatted excitedly about their first tennis practice coming up right after school. Becca admitted that she was a little nervous. Chloe and Ranju had played together in a tennis camp over the summer and both felt more confident than Becca. It was during the summer tennis camp that Chloe and Ranju became friends. Chloe remarked, "Ranju will surely be the best one on the team! She did great at camp!" She also encouraged Becca, "Just have fun. You'll learn a lot from watching Ranju."

Tennis practice went great that afternoon and all the girls had a lot of fun. Chloe went home with Ranju after practice because her parents were both working late that night. They wouldn't be picking her up until at least 7:00pm, so Ranju's mom asked Chloe if she wanted to join them for dinner. She didn't want to be rude so after some hesitation, she said, "Sure. It looks really good!"

Ranju's mom was wearing a beautiful dress, and Chloe asked Ranju if she always wore such pretty clothes. Ranju explained that her mom was wearing a sari. Ranju showed Chloe some of her mom's other colorful silk saris and explained that they were traditional to the Indian culture. Chloe thought they were the most beautiful clothes she had ever seen.

Chloe couldn't believe how good the curried vegetables with rice was. She was amazed that she ate an entire dinner that didn't include any meat. She also couldn't wait to tell her parents that she ate a whole meal without using a fork or spoon. She used bread instead. Something that Ranju had called naan. And for dessert, she had gulab jamun. She had never tasted anything like it in her life!

The next day at school, Chloe told Becca and her other friends all about how cool Ranju's customs were. She told them about the saris, what she learned about Hinduism, and all about the great food and how everyone in Ranju's family was a vegetarian. Because of Chloe taking the time to learn about and appreciate Ranju's cultural differences, Ranju felt accepted and respected and was no longer embarrassed that she was different than Chloe and some of the other kids.

LET'S DISCUSS

1   What did Chloe do to be a culturally sensitive leader?

2   What may have happened if Chloe hadn't taken the time to learn about and accept Ranju's customs?

3   How do you think Ranju felt because of Chloe taking the time to learn about her cultural traditions and customs?

4   How might Chloe sharing what she learned about Ranju's customs with others affect how others treat Ranju?

5   In what ways can you be a culturally sensitive leader to others who have different cultural traditions and beliefs than you?

LEADERSHIP LEARNING ACTIVITY

Put together a menu for breakfast, lunch, and dinner. Share something that you commonly eat for each meal and then share something that is eaten in another culture for breakfast, lunch, and dinner. If you don't have an example from another culture, research or ask someone who is from a different culture what they commonly eat for each meal.

WHAT'S ON THE MENU?

Breakfast

Yours: _____

Theirs: _____

Lunch

Yours: _____

Theirs: _____

Dinner

Yours: _____

Theirs: _____

DAVID
THE DEPENDABLE LEADER

"Trust is earned by following through
and being dependable in small
things as well as in large things."

UNKNOWN AUTHOR

DEFINITION

Dependable Leader – Others can count on you to do what you say
you are going to do.

WHAT IT MEANS FOR YOU

To be dependable is to be trustworthy and reliable. It means fulfilling
what is promised, even if it requires unexpected sacrifice. So whether
you are at home, at school, or on the playing field, when you are
dependable, others know they can count on you to fulfill your
commitment and do your part.

DAVID
THE DEPENDABLE LEADER

It seemed like an extra-long day at school. David and his friends kept looking out the window and wishing they could be outside playing in the beautiful early fall weather. The leaves were just starting to change color and it was the kind of day that you could ride your bike for hours without getting too hot or too cold.

Mr. Kasper was talking about the service activity that the class would be doing with the Busy Bee Preschool program. Mr. Kasper's entire fourth grade class was scheduled to read to the eight preschool classes next Thursday as part of a project on social responsibility and volunteering. David knew first hand about volunteering. His mom and dad volunteered to serve food at the homeless shelter at least once a month; and for the last two Thanksgiving holidays, he, his older brother Wyatt and his parents served turkey dinner at the shelter. It was actually kind of fun. All of the volunteers took turns sitting and eating part of the meal with those whom they served. For the last two years, David sat with a man named Ralph who spoke with a slow southern drawl and told of his early years playing baseball and later working on a clam boat. David loved Ralph's stories.

"I wonder where Ralph is now?" David thought to himself. His thought was interrupted by the end-of-school bell. The kids all jumped up, grabbed their backpacks and were off to the races! An actual race, that is! David and his friends planned to race their bikes all the way home to each of their houses and the one to get their bat and glove and get to the park first would be the winner and the one who would pitch for their fiercely competitive neighborhood homeroom derby. David knew he had this one in the bag! Unless, of course, his mom made him stop and tell her all about his day. He didn't have a moment to lose. Mom would have to wait. When he got home, he gave her a quick kiss on the cheek and promised to tell her about his day later and he was off!

David couldn't believe it. Bobby Holden beat him to the park! "Oh well. I guess I'll just have to win the actual homerun derby," he thought. His friends had a blast and each of them had a few great hits. In the end, Eddie McNabb won the derby. He was the only one to hit it off the Trident Bank sign in center field. The boys talked about Eddie's hit all the way home and tried to guess who would be the first one to hit it clear out of the park.

The week went by fast and the Busy Bee volunteer day was awesome! The fourth graders missed a half day of school to volunteer. They were adored by all the preschoolers, and to boot, got free popsicles from the teachers at the Busy Bee. One of the teachers overheard David telling Bobby, "Volunteering is great! I wish we could do this every week!"

Miss Kathy chimed in, "Well, as a matter of fact, you can do it every week if you want. We are looking for regular volunteers to come after school for one hour every week to read and spend time with some of our special needs children. David, I think you met Joanie earlier today. She is one of our students who requires a little extra attention and her love for reading is one of the reasons we are starting this new program."

David thanked Miss Kathy for letting him know about the opportunity and promised he would talk it over with his parents before giving her an answer. As he told his parents about it during dinner that night, they told him how proud they were of him for even considering volunteering once a week. They also reminded him of the importance of following through when making a big commitment like this.

David stopped by the preschool the next day and told Miss Kathy that he was ready to volunteer and was committed to come every Thursday for the next two months. He explained that basketball would be starting after that and he would have to see which day practices would be so he could figure out if he would be able to keep volunteering.

David came to the preschool the next two Thursdays and really enjoyed his time with Joanie and a little fuzzy-haired boy named Derrick. Miss Kathy told him how much they looked forward to seeing him every Thursday and how much she appreciated his dedication to the after-school program.

At school, the day after David's second visit to the preschool, Bobby and Kyle nearly tackled David as they shared the exciting news that a few of the players from the high school baseball team had heard about their neighborhood homerun derby and wanted to come and do a hitting clinic for the kids and participate in the homerun derby next Thursday.

"That's awesome!" David exclaimed. He then remembered that he volunteered on Thursdays and told his friends he wasn't sure what to do.

They couldn't believe David was thinking about choosing preschool kids over baseball! "I'm sure they will understand if you skip one week!" Bobby pleaded. "Just tell them you're sick," urged Kyle.

David just picked at his plate of food that night at dinner. He didn't know if he should tell his parents what was wrong. "I know what they'll say," he thought.

When he finally admitted to them what was going on, he was surprised at their reaction. His dad said, "Sounds like you have a tough decision to make, son."

His mom patted him on the hand and said, "We know you'll think this through and we support whatever you decide."

David was so glad to hear that he wouldn't disappoint his parents if he chose to play baseball over volunteering next week. He then thought about Joanie and Derrick and how disappointed they might be though. "And what about my promise to Miss Kathy?" David worried.

He told Bobby and Kyle his decision at school the next day. They were disappointed and didn't understand why he took his volunteering job so seriously but were impressed that he was always so dependable. Everyone knew that they could always count on David to follow through on his commitments and promises.

LET'S DISCUSS

1 What did David do to demonstrate he was a dependable leader?

2 What may have happened if David decided to play baseball rather than stick to his commitment at the preschool?

3 How may David's actions have influenced his friends?

4 Are there any other solutions to David's dilemma?

5 What can you do to demonstrate that you are a dependable leader?

LEADERSHIP LEARNING ACTIVITY

Answer the following trivia questions about being a dependable leader.

Question 1

Which one of the following best describes someone who is dependable?

a)   usually late

b)   doesn't show up

c)   always on time

d)   goes fishing instead

Question 2

As a dependable leader, if you make a commitment to do something, you:

a)   keep your commitment

b)   tell jokes after you miss your commitment

c)   make excuses for why you can't come

d)   blame others when you can't complete your commitment

Question 3

Which one of the following best describes someone who is dependable?

a)   can always be counted on to follow through on their commitment

b)   shows up on time

c)   puts others' needs above their own

d)   all of the above

Answers: Question 1: c)   Question 2: a)   Question 3: d)

ENZO
THE ENCOURAGING LEADER

"If your actions inspire others to
dream more, learn more, do more
and become more, you are a leader."

JOHN QUINCY ADAMS

DEFINITION

Encouraging Leader – You use kind words to give others courage,
hope, or confidence.

WHAT IT MEANS FOR YOU

When you are encouraging, you go out of your way to build up other
people. You say things that you know will encourage others to do
more and be more than they would have otherwise. You recognize
that everyone needs encouragement. Sometimes it's little words of
encouragement that help someone get through a rough day. Sometimes
a small amount of encouragement can make a big difference in the life
of a classmate or friend.

ENZO
THE ENCOURAGING LEADER

"Man you can play that trumpet!" Enzo said to a kid named Mark Herman.

"Nah, I stink," replied Mark. "My dad says I sound like a dying goose," he sighed.

It was Mark's first year in the band and he was nervous that he wouldn't be able to catch on as quickly as the majority of the other kids who played last year. Actually, Mark assumed that he would fail at the trumpet just like he failed at soccer, baseball, and everything else he tried. At least that's what his dad told him all the time. His dad reminded him every chance he could how he kicked the ball in the wrong goal at his first soccer game and how he struck out all the time in baseball and caused the team to lose. "I don't know why I even bother," Mark thought.

Enzo interrupted his thoughts: "I sounded much worse than a dying goose when I first started. I believe I made sounds closer to that of an elephant passing gas."

That made Mark laugh a little. Mark shrugged and said, "I guess it doesn't matter what I sound like. I'm stuck doing it. My mom won't let me quit until I try it for at least one month."

Enzo smiled at Mark and said, "Well then, that gives me a month to convince you to stay. I bet if you stick with it, you'll move up to first chair trumpet by January."

Mark had no idea why Enzo would say such a thing. "I'll be lucky if I learn the right finger positions, let alone be able to play a song by then," he thought.

When band practice was over, Mr. Price reminded them, "Practice daily, at least 30 minutes a day. But make sure that you do some warm ups before you jump into the songs. You have to keep your chops warm, otherwise you will lose your consistency." On his way out, Mr. Price handed Mark a fingering chart to help him at home.

"Let me know if you want to practice together tomorrow after school?" asked Enzo. "Rick usually comes over to my house to practice but he's getting his braces on tomorrow and can't come. It will give us an extra day to work on the scales and your finger placement."

At Enzo's house the next day, Mark was getting frustrated when he couldn't play the scales perfectly. "Be patient," Enzo stressed. "Trust me, it'll come with practice. Every day of practice gives the goose another day of life!" They both laughed.

"We'll practice again tomorrow. I think Rick will be able to come over, too. Why don't we take a break and play on the Wii until your mom comes to pick you up?" asked Enzo.

The three boys practiced together over the next several weeks. Rick was having a hard time because of his braces. Enzo always did his best but was not a natural musician like Rick and Mark. Mark was beginning to really get the hang of the trumpet and the band teacher was very impressed with how quickly he picked up the songs. Mark's personal one-month obligation to the band came and went without him even thinking about it.

In early December, Mr. Price was assigning the chairs for each of the instruments and because of Rick still having difficulty playing with braces on, he asked Mark if he felt ready to be first chair trumpet for the Holiday Band Concert.

Mark was thrilled and couldn't wait to tell his mom.

The only thing his dad said was "Make sure you don't screw up and embarrass me like usual."

He started to doubt himself and believe his dad may be right. "I have screwed up at everything I've ever tried," he thought.

At band practice, he wasn't hitting the notes like he had been the previous couple of practices. "What's wrong?" Enzo asked.

"I just can't do this!" Mark complained. "I'm not good enough to be playing first chair!"

Enzo reminded him, "Mr. Price would not have asked you to be first chair if he didn't think you were good enough. I have been practicing with you a couple times a week for the last two months and I know how good you are and that you deserve to be here! Don't doubt yourself. You're a great trumpet player with a ton of natural talent. You can do this!"

The holiday band concert was great. Mr. Price was so pleased with how well they did. They all played their best but Mark's trumpet solo was the highlight of the night.

Mark's mom gave him the biggest hug of his life, and whispered to him, "I am so proud of you."

His dad didn't say anything. "I guess that's better than him saying something negative," Mark thought.

Rick and Enzo told him how awesome he did and asked Mark and his parents if they wanted to come with their families to Luigi's for some pizza to celebrate.

Mark never felt so happy. He was so glad that he had these new friends, and was especially thankful that Enzo had kept encouraging him to play the trumpet. Because of Enzo, he finally had something in his life that he was proud of.

LET'S DISCUSS

1. Why was Mark so hard on himself all the time?

2. What were a few of the specific things Enzo said to encourage Mark?

3. How may Enzo's words and actions have actually changed Mark's life?

4. Can you think of a time someone said encouraging words to you? If so, how did that make you feel?

5. What are some things you can say or do today to be an encouraging leader to someone else?

LEADERSHIP LEARNING ACTIVITY

Write a letter to thank someone who has been encouraging to you. Share what he or she did to encourage you and why it meant so much to you.

Dear _____

_____

_____

_____

_____

_____

_____

_____

_____

_____

_____

Thank you for your encouragement

_____

FIONA
THE FAIR LEADER

"In all things: Do unto others as you would have them do unto you."

THE GOLDEN RULE

DEFINITION
Fair Leader – You understand and follow rules, and apply them equally to everyone.

WHAT IT MEANS FOR YOU
Fairness is knowing and following the rules and understanding that rules apply equally to everyone. This can be accomplished by taking turns, listening, and sharing with others. It is also accomplished by not showing favor to any one person above another. When you are fair to others, it allows everyone an equal chance to be involved and succeed. Always remember the Golden Rule and treat others the way that you want to be treated.

FIONA
THE FAIR LEADER

Fiona and her friend Jasmine Hernandez skipped and laughed the whole way into their first Girl Scout meeting of the year.

"I wonder if there will be anybody new this year?" asked Fiona.

Jasmine playfully pushed Fiona and said, "I don't know, but we are not sharing our secret 'cookie-selling' spot with anyone else!"

As they walked into the meeting room, they recognized a few of their friends from last year as well as some new faces. They said hi to Angela and Addison Mosser, the twins from the other fourth grade class in their school, as well as to Monique Alfonso and Jane Sutter. They also smiled at Shilpa Mehta, who was from their class but new to Girl Scouts, and at another new girl that they had never seen before.

Mary Lopez, the scout leader, asked the girls to sit down and go around the table and introduce themselves.

Jasmine went first and was sure to mention that she was one of the original Girl Scouts of Troop #7404.

Fiona rolled her eyes at her friend and then introduced herself and shared that this was her third year as well, and that she was really excited about the troop earning money for another great trip this year.

Angela and Addison said it was their second year and they couldn't wait to earn more badges and sell the most cookies in the troop this year!

Jasmine made eye contact with Fiona and crossed her arms.

Monique introduced herself and said she couldn't wait to see all the new crafts they would be doing.

Jane was shy as usual and only gave her name and wouldn't say anything else.

Shilpa said this was her first year and that she didn't know much about Girl Scouts but that her mom was in a troop when she was a little girl and thought Shilpa should try it.

The other new girl introduced herself as Maddie Tonko and said she was homeschooled and was looking forward to making new friends.

Mary then went over the contents of the green folders sitting in front of each of the girls. She explained, "There are certain rules and laws that we follow in the troop and there will be no exceptions. The most important one is the Girl Scout Law. I would like each of you to recite it. Read along on page two if you don't know it by heart."

I will do my best to be:

Honest and Fair

Friendly and Helpful

Considerate and Caring

Courageous and Strong

Responsible for what I say and do

Respect myself and others

Respect authority

Use resources wisely

Make the world a better place

And be a sister to every Girl Scout.

Mary then had the girls break up into two teams to do a scavenger hunt. Each team had to find five of their own colored clues hidden throughout the meeting room and in the gym next door and bring them back to unscramble a word. Jasmine, Fiona, Monique, and Maddie were on the red team, and Angela, Addison, Jane, and Shilpa were on the blue team. The girls raced around to get each of the clues.

When Jasmine saw the last of the blue team's clues, she said to Fiona, "Let's put their last clue in my bag to make sure we win."

Fiona stopped and stared at her friend. "Jasmine, how would you like it if they did that to us? We need to play by the rules."

The blue team finished first and came back with their clues, which included the letters O, E, T, A, R, and the red team finished with the letters H, N, S, F, I. Neither team could figure out what their scrambled word was.

Mary offered them a hint. "Why don't your two teams work on it together?" They still couldn't figure it out and she offered them one last hint: "Why don't you try to combine all of the letters from the two teams?"

It took a little while, but the girls finally realized that the unscrambled words alternated red and blue letters, and were "honest" and "fair."

LET'S DISCUSS

1. Why do you think the scout leader, Mary, had the girls do this scavenger hunt and word scramble?

2. What could have happened if Fiona hadn't reminded Jasmine to play fair and by the rules?

3. How may Jasmine's actions have affected how the new girls felt about Girl Scouts?

4. Why is it important to always play fairly and by the rules?

5. Can you think of a time when either you or another person acted as a fair leader and how it affected the situation?

LEADERSHIP LEARNING ACTIVITY

Unscramble the phrase on the next page and then share what the unscrambled phrase means to you.

HTE OLGDNE ULRE

___   _____   ____

What does the unscrambled phrase mean to you?

_____

_____

_____

_____

_____

_____

_____

GABE
THE GRATEFUL LEADER

> "Begin each day with
> a grateful heart."

UNKNOWN AUTHOR

DEFINITION

Grateful Leader – You are thankful to others and show them that you appreciate them.

WHAT IT MEANS FOR YOU

When you are grateful, you say or do things to show others that you are thankful and appreciate them. For example, you send a thank you card when someone gives you a birthday or holiday gift. You recognize and thank others when they do something for you. You try not to take people or things for granted and are thankful for what you have.

GABE
THE GRATEFUL LEADER

As Gabe and his dad walked to the car, he heard his dad say to their neighbor, "Hey Frank, thanks so much for blowing the leaves off our driveway yesterday. I've been so busy with work that I haven't had much time to take care of the yard work. I really appreciate your help."

On the way to school, Gabe told his dad all about the model rocket competition that the gifted club entered. He explained that they needed to raise the money themselves for the entry fee, supplies, and travel expenses to get to the competition.

His dad reminded him about all the overtime he was working just to pay the bills and that they didn't have any extra money right now to give toward things like that.

"It's okay, Dad. We'll figure something out," said Gabe.

During their meeting before school, Gabe and his three friends talked about the cool rocket that they would design for the competition and how they could raise the money to get there.

Brad Hurley and Suresh Kumar said that each of their parents would help a little but expected them to raise most of the money themselves.

Sam Johnson said his parents were willing to help by driving them the 300 miles to the competition.

"Well, that's a start," Gabe said with a smile. He thought about his own parents and his earlier conversation with his dad about them not being able to give anything toward the competition. His thoughts drifted back to his dad being thankful for their nice neighbor, Frank, who helped with some of their yard work. "I have a great idea," Gabe said excitedly. "We should ask our family and neighbors if they want to give anything toward the competition, and to show our appreciation, we can ask them what we can do to help them around their houses or yards."

Everyone agreed that they would spend at least one hour showing their appreciation to anyone who contributed.

The four friends raised all the money that they needed within three weeks. It was mainly because Mr. Bob Williams, Gabe's older, blind neighbor, gave generously. He gave even though he had no yard and no work that needed to be done in his small apartment. Gabe knew he would have to come up with something special to show Mr. Williams his appreciation.

The competition was amazing! The teams all competed in three areas: hitting an exact altitude, launching and landing within a certain amount of time, and returning a raw egg ("the pilot") without cracking it. Gabe and his friends ended up taking third in the competition and brought home a bronze trophy in the shape of a rocket.

When they got home from the competition, they showed each of their families their trophy and excitedly told them all about the cool rocket designs they saw and what they would do differently next year to win first place in the competition. Gabe also had one more stop he wanted to make. The friends all agreed that to show their biggest supporter how grateful they were for his donation, they would give Mr. Williams their rocket trophy.

LET'S DISCUSS

1. How did the kids show their appreciation to their family and neighbors?

2. How do you think Mr. Williams felt about the kids wanting to give him their trophy?

3. Why is it important to show others that you appreciate them?

4. Can you think of a time when someone showed you how grateful he or she was for your help? How did that make you feel?

5. What are some ways that you can be a grateful leader?

LEADERSHIP LEARNING ACTIVITY

You have the opportunity to give someone a trophy to show how grateful you are to him or her. Write the person's name on the trophy and tell him or her why you are grateful.

To:

_____

I'm grateful to

you because:

_____

_____

_____

_____

HUNTER
THE HONEST LEADER

> "Honesty is the first chapter
> in the book of wisdom."

THOMAS JEFFERSON

DEFINITION

Honest Leader – You always tell the truth.

WHAT IT MEANS FOR YOU

When you are honest, you can be counted on to tell the whole truth about a situation. You can be trusted to not cheat, lie, cover up a wrong, or steal. You have the integrity to admit when you have made a mistake, even if you might get into trouble for it. You also avoid saying things about people that are not true.

HUNTER
THE HONEST LEADER

Hunter and his older brother, Joey, had been playing in their tree fort for over two hours before they remembered that they had promised to do their chores and homework before dinner.

"Time to eat!" called their mom.

"Mom is going to be so mad at us!" cried Hunter.

"We'll sneak in the garage door, take out the trash quick, and tell her that we already did our homework on the bus," suggested Joey.

"Well I did do some of my homework on the bus, so I guess it's kind of the truth," thought Hunter.

During dinner, their dad asked, "How was your day at school, boys?"

Joey replied first. "It was great. We had a substitute and she had no clue what we were supposed to be doing so we let her do the same lesson that Mrs. Frey taught us yesterday."

"Did it occur to any one of you to help her out and let her know what lesson you were supposed to be doing?" their dad said with raised eyebrows.

"Hunter, how was your day?" his mom interjected.

Hunter replied, "Umm, it was good. I brought home my math and spelling tests that need to be signed. Mr. Pack also told us that we have a unit test in science on Friday."

"Did you study as part of your homework tonight?" his mom asked.

Joey glared at Hunter to make sure he didn't give away their secret.

"Yep, all done," Hunter said with a nervous smile.

Their dad then announced that he had four tickets for the big Bristol College football game this weekend. "So make sure you listen to your mom this week and help her around the house with the chores so we can leave early on Saturday for the game," he said.

After they helped clear the table and took their plates to the sink, Hunter and Joey went outside to play basketball for a little while before they had to get ready for bed.

"Make sure you don't say anything to screw up our chance to go to the game this weekend!" Joey scolded.

As Hunter was lying in bed, his mom walked in to his room and he didn't have time to shove his unfinished homework back in his bag. "I almost forgot to sign your tests," his mom said. As she reached for his folder, she saw his unfinished homework and asked about it.

He stumbled for words and said, "It's just extra stuff. I didn't really need to do it."

His mom looked straight at him and asked if he was telling the truth.

He thought about what his brother had said to him about not screwing up their chance to go to the game, but he just couldn't lie anymore. He swallowed hard and said, "I'm really sorry, mom. We forgot to do all of our chores and homework before dinner and I lied to you about it."

His mom hesitated, and then said, "Well, I'm really disappointed that you lied to me but I am very glad that you told me the truth now. I'm sorry but there will be no game this weekend for you and your brother. However, had I found this out without you telling me, the consequences would have been much worse than just missing the game."

Hunter sighed. "I'm upset about the game and how angry Joey is going to be, but I'm really glad I told you the truth."

As his mom walked out, she said, "Good night, son. I'm very proud of you for admitting you made a mistake and being honest about it. Now let's see what your brother has to say."

LET'S DISCUSS

1. Why do you think Hunter told more than one lie?

2. What could the boys have done differently to avoid feeling the need to lie?

3. How do you think Hunter and Joey's parents felt about the boys lying?

4. Why is telling the truth so important?

5. Can you think of a time when someone lied to you? How did that made you feel?

LEADERSHIP LEARNING ACTIVITY

Look at the following list of choices and circle the smiley face ☺ if it is a good choice and the frowny face ☹ if it is a poor choice.

You tell only the truth   ☺ ☹

You trick someone   ☺ ☹

You steal a piece of candy   ☺ ☹

You return a found item   ☺ ☹

You cheat on a test   ☺ ☹

You say what you mean   ☺ ☹

You tell the whole truth   ☺ ☹

You tell a lie about a bully   ☺ ☹

You exaggerate the truth   ☺ ☹

You apologize for a mistake   ☺ ☹

ISABELLA
THE INNOVATIVE LEADER

"There's a way to do it better - find it."

THOMAS EDISON

DEFINITION

Innovative Leader — You come up with new ideas.

WHAT IT MEANS FOR YOU

When you are innovative, you look for new, creative ways to make improvements. You try to add value to whatever you do. You also understand that it is better to try something and fail than to not try at all. You look to learn from others' and your own mistakes.

ISABELLA
THE INNOVATIVE LEADER

Isabella smiled to herself as she separated and dumped her lunch tray into the three different cans: recycling, trash, and compost. She had submitted the idea to add compost cans to the cafeteria last year after she and her family visited a working eighteenth-century farm the previous summer. While at the farm, she learned that in the old days, they made use of everything they had and didn't let anything go to waste. Even the scraps of food from visitors' lunches were used to feed the hogs. What the hogs didn't eat was used as compost material on the farm. Because the high school had an agriculture program that worked with local farms, Isabella suggested that they use the elementary, middle, and high schools' lunch compost to help with recycling efforts and to help fertilize the county farms. The school district didn't want to be bothered at first but she persisted in her efforts with both the school board and several of the local farmers, and both groups finally agreed that her idea was one worth thinking about. Six months later, there were three different cans in every lunch room throughout the school district.

This year, she had a more personal improvement on her mind. The principal announced at their last assembly that the school's winter and spring musicals might need to be canceled because they couldn't find money in the budget this year to rebuild the stage, buy new props, and replace the torn curtains from last year's storm damage. The school board decided that it was just too dangerous for the kids to use the stage this year.

Isabella frowned. "The musicals are the highlight of my year," she thought. She decided that she would have to talk to some of the other kids and come up with a plan to save the musicals.

She asked several of the kids who were in the musicals last year if they could meet after school the next day to talk about the situation.

Like Isabella, most of the kids were disappointed but didn't have a clue what to do about it. One of Isabella's friends, Abdu Ali, suggested that they try to use the town's community theater.

"That's a great idea!" Isabella agreed. She suggested that a few of them go talk to the theater's owner and find out if they could use it this year.

"I'm so sorry, kids. The theater is already being used every night of the week," Mr. Elmer, the theater owner, told them. "I'll sure miss coming to see your musicals this year," he remarked.

"Back to the drawing board," Isabella said as they walked out.

The kids said good-bye to one another and agreed to talk about it again tomorrow.

Isabella thought about the situation the whole night. She was day dreaming about how good it felt last year when the compost idea finally got approved. That's when the idea came to her. "Instead of replacing the stage and curtains and buying new props, we can try to reuse what we already have, possibly borrow some props from Mr. Elmer, and ask some of the adults in the community to help repair the stage and sew the curtain." Her Aunt Millie was a great seamstress and Isabella knew she would want to help.

Isabella and her friends talked to Mr. Elmer the next day and he was more than happy to let the kids borrow some of the props that weren't currently being used. Aunt Millie offered not only to repair the torn curtain, but to add some additional embellishments to make it look even better than before. Richie Parker's dad owned a hardware store and offered to help with the lumber and repairs of the stage. The school board was so impressed with the efforts of the kids and their creativity in solving the problem that they just couldn't say no.

The winter musical was a huge success. Everyone who helped with the project was there with VIP front row seats. Each of the members of the school board came and several of them remarked to Isabella afterwards that they were so glad that she was persistent in coming up with an innovative solution to make this great program happen. They couldn't wait to see how good the spring musical would be!

LET'S DISCUSS

1. In what way may Isabella have influenced other kids in her school?

2. Why is it important to think of more than one solution to a problem?

3. Why is it better to try something and fail at it than not try at all?

4. Why is it important to be an innovative leader?

5. Is there any situation or problem in your life that you can think about to find a new or different innovative solution?

LEADERSHIP LEARNING ACTIVITY

Get those creative brain bulbs shining bright and use the sketch pad on the next page to draw or write about an innovative idea that you have thought about. Draw or describe how your idea will fix or improve an existing problem. Be creative – think outside the box to fix an issue at school or at home, or a flaw with one of your toys, or just describe a great idea you have for a future product.

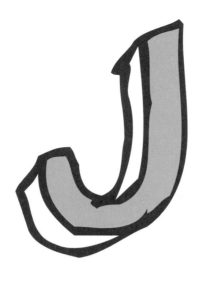

JAIDA
THE JUST LEADER

"The struggle for peace includes the struggle for freedom and justice for the masses of all countries."

ARTHUR HENDERSON

DEFINITION

Just Leader – You show fairness and equality to others.

WHAT IT MEANS FOR YOU

When you are just, you believe in equality and fairness. You try to respect, cooperate with, and listen to others knowing it will lead to better friendships and positive relationships with others. You try to do what is best for everyone. You stand up for those being treated unfairly.

JAIDA
THE JUST LEADER

Jaida and her friend Molly Arnold were walking down the hall talking about their upcoming book report.

"What are you thinking about doing it on?" asked Jaida.

"Oh, I don't know, maybe I'll find a book on pickled vegetables or why knees are shaped so weird!" Molly teased.

"Ha ha, very funny," said Jaida. "You know this book report is due in one week and you are not taking it very seriously," she scolded.

"I know. Mrs. Ernesto said to do it on something or someone that we consider impactful. The only thing that is impactful to me is a good joke."

"Well, that's what you should do it on then," encouraged Jaida.

"Maybe you're right. I'll try to find a good book about comedians. If that doesn't work out, there's always the pickled vegetables!" Molly joked. The girls both laughed.

Jaida looked in the school library briefly and couldn't find a book that she really connected with. "I'll have to have mom take me to the public library tomorrow," she thought.

That night as they were eating their pizza, Jaida told her mom she was having trouble finding a book that was impactful to her for her upcoming book report.

"Well, only you can decide that. You have always liked reading about people who have impacted history. Why don't you look at some of the books written about people who have made a major difference in the world?" her mom asked.

"Not a bad idea," said Jaida.

As she flipped through various biography books, Jaida considered ones on Emelia Earhart, Albert Einstein, and Mother Teresa. "They are all impactful, just not to me personally," she thought. She went down one more shelf and knew as soon as she saw it. "Martin Luther King, Jr.!" she exclaimed. As a young black person, she knew the impact that Martin Luther King, Jr. had on the creation of civil rights and equality for all. She remembered her grandfather talking about King receiving the Nobel Peace Prize in 1964 for combating racial inequality through nonviolence. This was definitely a person who impacted her and a book she could proudly give a report on.

Jaida began her book report by quoting Martin Luther King, Jr.: "But we come here tonight to be saved from that patience that makes us patient with anything less than freedom and justice." She explained, "To me, this means not putting up with people who are unfair and disrespect others because they are different. I want to be someone who stands up for others who aren't treated fairly." Jaida ended her report by stating that, "Dr. King wanted freedom and equality to replace slavery and hatred. King was a symbol of justice, and I, for one, will try hard every day to live out the very things that he stood for."

LET'S DISCUSS

1. Why do you think Jaida picked a biography on Martin Luther King, Jr. for her book report?

2. What stood out to you the most about Martin Luther King, Jr.?

3. How may Jaida's book report influence others?

4. Why is it so important to be a fair and just leader?

5. In what ways can you be a fair and just leader to others?

LEADERSHIP LEARNING ACTIVITY

Martin Luther King, Jr. spoke about the importance of freedom and justice. If you had to give a speech on something that is important to you, what would it be? Give your speech a title and write a few sentences about your topic.

Title:

_____

_____

_____

_____

_____

_____

_____

_____

_____

_____

_____

_____

KEVIN
THE KIND LEADER

"Be kind, for everyone you meet
is fighting a hard battle."

PLATO

DEFINITION

Kind Leader – You are caring and compassionate to others.

WHAT IT MEANS FOR YOU

When you are kind, you care about others and try to do nice things for them. You are willing to help others and often think of others before you think of yourself. You can show kindness to others by giving a compliment, listening to someone, lending a pencil, letting someone go in front of you, opening the door for someone, and sitting with someone new at lunch.

KEVIN
THE KIND LEADER

Kevin liked helping Mrs. Longacre straighten up the room before the end of the day. She often gave him a twizzler or tootsie roll for being kind and helpful.

As he was walking out, she reminded him that the new student, Ben Andrews, would be starting tomorrow. She had mentioned it to the class earlier in the week and asked if anyone would be willing to show Ben around the school. Kevin had happily volunteered. He liked meeting new kids, and besides, he was hoping to have another friend to play soccer with.

Mrs. Longacre had said, "Thank you for volunteering, Kevin." She continued telling the class, "So that you are not surprised, I want you to be aware that Ben is in a wheelchair. It's my understanding that he can manage just fine by himself but I want you to be willing to help him with things if he asks." The class had a lot of questions about Ben, but Mrs. Longacre simply replied, "Just treat him like anyone else. I've heard great things about him and I think you are really going to like him."

Kevin was sort of nervous about meeting Ben. He had never personally known anyone with a physical disability. Kevin loved running around and playing tag and doing all kinds of sports and wasn't sure if he would have anything in common to talk about or do with Ben. "I just have to be nice to him," he thought.

When Ben rolled into the classroom, some of the kids stared at his wheelchair and didn't even say hi to him. A few others quickly said hello but became very quiet. Kevin forgot all about his own worries, walked up to Ben to introduce himself, and said, "Nice to meet you. Welcome to our class."

After Mrs. Longacre had each of the other kids introduce themselves, she asked Kevin to show Ben around the school.

Kevin enjoyed getting to know Ben as they toured the school. When Kevin showed him the playground, Ben remarked, "Do you guys like to play tag? I might have an unfair advantage being so lightning fast in this chair but I'll give you a head start if you want."

Kevin teased back and said, "I'll just make sure I'm on your team!" Kevin then admitted to Ben that he had been a little nervous about what types of things he would be able to do. "What other things do you like to do?" Kevin asked.

"Probably the same kinds of things you like to do," Ben said. "I just might have a harder time doing it, but that doesn't stop me from wanting to try," he continued.

When they were almost back to the classroom, Kevin asked, "Can we make a deal? I will try to treat you the same as everyone else if you agree that if there is something special that you want or need, you'll tell me. I don't want to exclude you or hurt your feelings on purpose but I don't want you to feel bad if we are doing something that you can't or don't want to do."

Ben responded, "You got it! I think that's the most honest, kind thing anyone has ever said to me. Thanks for being a friend and asking what I want and not just pitying me like most people do. I think I'm really going to like it here."

LET'S DISCUSS

1. What did Kevin do to show Ben kindness?

2. Why was Ben so surprised at Kevin's kindness?

3. How might Kevin's actions toward Ben influence the other kids to treat him?

4. Why is it important to be kind to others?

5. Share an example of when you did something kind for another person.

LEADERSHIP LEARNING ACTIVITY

Use the following table to write three more kind things you can do for others. On the left, write for whom you will do a kind gesture. On the right, describe the kind thing that you can do for the other person.

Who	Kind Thing to Do
Your parent	You fold the laundry and take out the trash without being asked because you know it has been a busy week at work.

LILLY
THE LISTENING LEADER

"Listen without interrupting."

PROVERBS 18:13

Listening Leader – You pay attention to what others say.

When you listen to others, you pay attention so that you understand what they are saying. When others talk, you look them in the eyes, you don't interrupt them, and you ask questions if you don't understand something that was said. When you are a good listener, you are able to follow directions the first time they are given.

LILLY
THE LISTENING LEADER

Lilly could hardly focus on what her teacher was saying because she was so excited that her grandmother was coming with her to her horseback riding lesson after school. She would have to introduce her grandmother to her favorite pony, Murphey, to Lance, the black stallion in the upper stall, and to her favorite barn cat, and show her how to groom and tack the horses.

Mrs. Samuel's voice chimed in, "Does anyone have any questions about what needs to be done for your homework?"

Lilly was too embarrassed to raise her hand and ask the teacher to repeat the directions so she didn't say anything.

On the way to the bus, Lilly asked her friend, Maria Rodriquez, what she was doing after school. As Maria began to tell her, Lilly interrupted her and blurted out, "Did I tell you that you can come to watch my first horse show this Sunday?"

Maria was frustrated with Lilly and said, "Yes. But do you remember me talking about my stepsister's wedding this weekend? Remember that I am in the wedding and we have a bunch of relatives coming from out of town? It's kind of a big deal."

"Oh, that's right. Sorry, I forgot," Lilly said.

Maria shrugged and said, "It's okay. I know you are excited about your horse show. It's just that sometimes you don't really listen when others are talking."

On the way home from horseback riding, Lilly asked her grandmother, "Do you think I'm a bad listener?"

Her grandmother smiled and said, "Well, you are an excitable girl who has a lot of things to talk about. You have to remember, however, that when one person does all the talking, it's easy to miss out on important things that others have to say. Do you recall your horseback riding instructor telling you to get the show saddle instead of your normal practice saddle? She told you twice but you were so distracted by showing me around that you ended up putting on the wrong saddle and wasting a good amount of your practice time today by having to retack your horse with the right one."

"I guess you're right," Lilly sighed. "How do I become a better listener?" she asked.

Her grandmother told her, "Try to focus on what someone is saying by having good eye contact with the person speaking, ask questions if you don't understand, and never interrupt them. You should use good listening skills with everyone, including your teachers, family members, and friends."

When Lilly saw Maria on Monday morning, she asked, "How was the wedding and spending time with all your crazy cousins?"

Maria paused and said, "Aren't you going to tell me all about your horse show first?"

"I'll tell you after you tell me all about the wedding and if you tripped walking down the aisle and all that good stuff!"

As the girls talked about the weekend, Lilly realized how important it was to use good listening skills to show others that you care about them and what they have to say.

1. Why did Lilly have such a hard time listening?

2. How do you think it made Maria feel when Lilly interrupted her and never really listened to what she had to say?

3. At the end, how do you think it made Maria feel when Lilly asked her about the wedding and let her talk first?

4. What good listening skills did Lilly's grandmother share with her?

5. What types of things can you do to show others that you are a listening leader?

LEADERSHIP LEARNING ACTIVITY

Draw a line to match up the consequences of poor listening habits on the left with the better choices on the right.

Your best friend is tired of you trying to always finish her story and move on to what you have to say because you never let her finish.		Focus on the other person by using good eye contact.
Your teacher asks you if you heard what he said because you were focusing on what was going on outside the window rather than on him and his instructions.		Don't interrupt.
Your project partner had to repeat himself three times because you continually butted in and didn't let him complete his thought.		Ask questions if you don't understand.
You were distracted by your video game when your mom gave you instructions multiple times for turning off the oven for dinner. You were too embarrassed to ask and didn't turn the oven off on time and burnt the meal.		Listen more and talk less.

MATT
THE MISSION-
MINDED LEADER

"Projects are determined by missions; the project is great if it has a great mission."

ANTON PAVLOVICH CHEKHOV

DEFINITION

Mission-Minded Leader – You stay focused on the task at hand.

WHAT IT MEANS FOR YOU

When you are mission-minded, you stay focused and engaged on what you are trying to accomplish. You are organized and pay attention to the details to get the job done right. This means that you avoid distractions and remain focused and motivated until the task is done. You can use this kind of mission-minded thinking when you are working on homework or projects, cleaning your room, or playing a game.

MATT
THE MISSION-MINDED LEADER

"Matt, don't forget to take your laptop charger with you today," his mom reminded him.

"It's already in my bag," Matt said with a smile.

His mom knew he was always one step ahead of her, but she felt she needed to do the "mom thing" and remind him anyway. Matt was one of those unique kids who rarely needed any direction. He was responsible in doing his chores at home and even more so with his schoolwork.

"I hope Robbie Donavon and Sinna Patel remember to bring in their flash drives with their final part of the South Africa project. I sent them an email last night reminding them," Matt said.

"I'm sure they will. You are a great project leader and have had the team organized and prepared for this presentation all week," his mom assured him.

As promised, Robbie and Sinna had completed their final parts of the group project. The team had to put it all together in the morning before they presented it to the class later that afternoon. They only had one hour of prep time during class to work on the final touches of their presentation so Matt had them get started right away.

"Robbie, you downloaded a picture of the South African flag, and did slides on the history and current demographics, right?" asked Matt.

"Yep. But did you see the first game of the World Series last night?" asked Robbie.

"I only saw a few minutes of the game but my dad told me about it this morning. Hey, since we have less than an hour to finish up and go over each of our parts of the presentation, can we stay focused on putting the project together and talk about the game over lunch?" Matt suggested.

"Sure," Robbie agreed.

"Sinna, let's see what you have for the slides on natural resources and major industry and economic facts," Matt said.

After the presentation, their teacher asked Matt, Robbie, and Sinna if they would be willing to present their project on South Africa at the school assembly. "Each class will have one group present their project to the entire school. I am very impressed with how organized and thorough you were with this project. You really did a great job. I'd sure like your group to represent our class!" she exclaimed.

The boys felt great about representing the class.

"Thanks for keeping us focused," Robbie said to Matt.

Sinna agreed and added, "Yeah. Thanks, Matt. My parents will be so happy that we got an 'A' on this project and got selected to present it to the school. I may even be able to convince them to take me to the movies this weekend! I want to work on every project with you!"

LET'S DISCUSS

1 What kinds of things did Matt do to be a mission-minded leader with their project?

2 Why did their teacher select them to represent the class at the school assembly?

3 What may have happened if the group lost focus and spent too much time talking about the World Series game?

4 Why is it important to be mission-minded and focused on what you are trying to accomplish?

5 In what areas of your life could you be a more focused, mission-minded leader?

LEADERSHIP LEARNING ACTIVITY

You have been assigned to be the project manager of a group science project that is due in one week. Your group needs to select a large cat of prey, such as a lion, tiger or panther, and discuss its speed and movement, its hunting pattern and what it eats, and where it lives. Pretend you are writing an email to two of your friends, Omar and Sabrina, who are working on the project with you. How would you divide up the work and what would you say to keep the team on task and complete your mission as project manager?

NATALIE
THE NAVIGATING LEADER

> "Go confidently in the direction
> of your dreams! Live the
> life you have imagined!"

HENRY DAVID THOREAU

DEFINITION

Navigating Leader – You put a plan in place to achieve your goals.

WHAT IT MEANS FOR YOU

When you are a navigating leader, you are intentional about the direction you take to achieve your goals. You think before you act and you stay on the path that leads you to your goal. You can navigate through tough situations and obstacles that could block you from achieving your goal.

NATALIE
THE NAVIGATING LEADER

"This is the hardest dismount I have ever tried," Natalie nervously said to her friend, Sarah Webster.

"You can do it! You nailed your layout step-out on the beam. You can do this," Sarah said, trying to encourage her friend.

"You're right. Here I go," Natalie whispered.

She twisted her body perfectly but landed hard and flew backwards onto her butt. Her coach, Michelle Michaels, walked over and gave her a hand to help her get up and said, "You're close. It'll come with practice. You've only been working on this new dismount for three weeks. Look how far you've come with your routines on the uneven bars and floor exercise."

"Yes, but the Regional Championships are in two weeks," Natalie said with concern.

As Natalie lay in bed that night, she thought about how much she wanted to win first place in the all-around division at the Regional Gymnastics Competition. "I have a really good chance. I have worked hard but I need to put a plan in place to work even harder without falling behind on my schoolwork the next two weeks," she thought. "I'll have to ask Mom and Dad if they would take me to the gym a few mornings before school and allow me to stay at practice for an extra hour every night."

"I'm not sure, Natalie. I think you are going to fall behind on homework or risk an injury before the competition," her dad said over breakfast the next morning.

Natalie pleaded with her father. "Dad, it's only an extra eight hours at the gym each week. She handed her dad a chart she had put together that morning showing what she needed to do over the next two weeks to stay on track to achieve her goal. "I'll talk to my teachers tomorrow morning about what assignments and tests I have over the next two weeks so I can plan ahead. I will do extra studying over lunch and before practice starts. I have never missed any homework before. I don't plan to start falling behind now. I just really need a few extra hours to practice each of the events before the competition."

Natalie worked very hard the next two weeks leading up to the competition. She stuck to her plan and stayed on top of her schoolwork and was totally focused and determined at practice.

At the Regionals, Coach Michaels pulled Natalie aside before she competed in her first event and said, "Your hard work has paid off. I've seen a big improvement in your strength, balance, and flexibility in all four of the events. You've stuck your beam dismount four out of the last five times. You're ready for the competition today. You have been a leader and an inspiration to the other girls. Now go show these judges that you deserve to be at the top of their leader board today!"

Natalie and another girl's scores were incredibly close after the first three events. The only event left was the balance beam. "I can do this. I've worked too hard to lose it now," Natalie thought. Sure enough, she nailed her routine and stuck her dismount perfectly.

After the scores were announced, her parents ran to her to congratulate her on winning the all-around division. As her dad hugged her, he said, "Natalie, I have never known a more determined person in my life. I am so proud of you for setting such high goals for yourself. You sure know what it takes to navigate your way to success."

LET'S DISCUSS

1. How did Natalie plan to achieve her goal of winning the all-around division at the Regional Gymnastics Competition?

2. Why do you think Coach Michaels felt Natalie was a leader for the other girls?

3. What may have happened if Natalie chose not to put a plan in place to stay on top of her schoolwork?

4. Why is it important to have a plan when you are trying to achieve a goal?

5. In what ways could you demonstrate that you are a navigating leader?

LEADERSHIP LEARNING ACTIVITY

Navigating leaders take the time to put a plan in place to reach their goals. As a navigating leader, what goal do you have (getting better grades, making a sports team, learning to play an instrument, spending more time with your family and less time on technology)? Put a plan in place by writing your goal in the large circle and then figuring out when you want to achieve your goal, what could prevent you from meeting your goal, and who is involved with your goal (friends, parents, teachers, coaches).

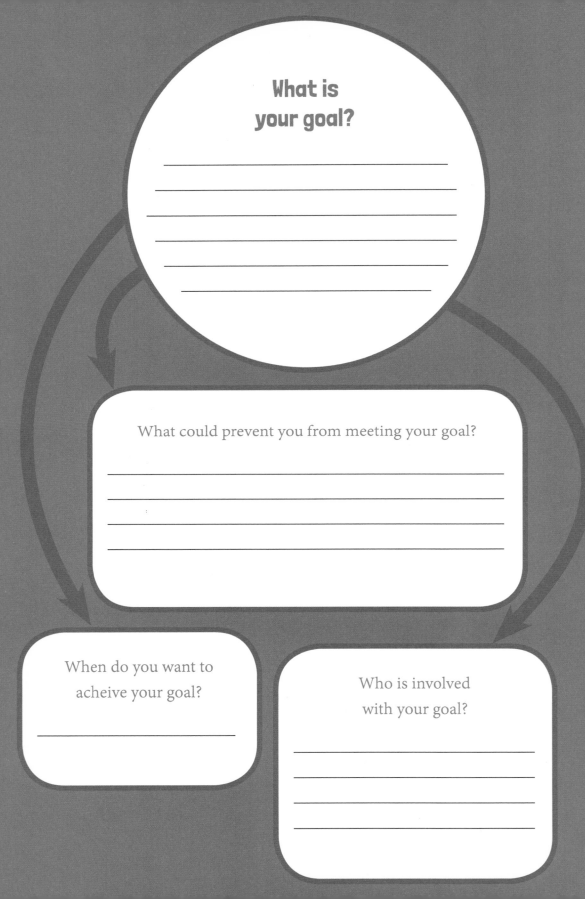

What is your goal?

_____
_____
_____
_____
_____
_____

What could prevent you from meeting your goal?

_____
_____
_____
_____

When do you want to acheive your goal?

_____

Who is involved with your goal?

_____
_____
_____
_____

OLIVIA
THE OPEN-MINDED LEADER

"An open mind leaves a chance for someone to drop a worthwhile thought in it."

MARK TWAIN

DEFINITION

Open-Minded Leader – You are willing to listen to other people's ideas.

WHAT IT MEANS FOR YOU

When you are an open-minded leader, you listen to other people's opinions and ideas and are willing to change your mind. You don't judge others for their choices and beliefs, and you treat everyone equally. You also encourage other people to accept and tolerate differences in others and be open-minded to what they suggest.

OLIVIA
THE OPEN-MINDED LEADER

It was a quiet Saturday afternoon and Olivia couldn't wait for her friends to come over for a playdate. She was excited that her two closest friends from dance class were going to meet her best friend from school. Maracelli West and Shayla Summers went to a different school and had never met April Hodges before. Olivia was hoping that everyone would get along.

"It's 2:00pm! Where is everyone?" Olivia worried.

"They'll be here soon," her mom replied. "April's mom texted me and said they'd be a few minutes late because her little brother had karate from 1:00pm to 2:00pm. I spoke to Maracelli's mom a few minutes ago confirming the directions. They're on their way," she reassured her.

Not a minute later the doorbell rang and Olivia ran to open the door for Maracelli and Shayla. The girls hugged each other and raced up to Olivia's bedroom.

"What do you think of our costumes for the dance recital?" asked Shayla.

"I don't know. I liked the blue one from last year much better. I think we look like cheetahs this year," said Maracelli.

"I think that's the point! We are supposed to be doing a scene from the Broadway show, *Cats*!" shrieked Shayla. The girls laughed.

Just then there was a knock on Olivia's open bedroom door and April popped her head in.

"Come in, silly," Olivia said to April. "I want you to meet Maracelli and Shayla."

She turned to the other girls, "And this is my friend, April, who I told you about." They all said hi.

"What do you guys want to do?" asked Olivia.

"I know," said Shayla excitedly. "Let's show April our recital dance."

April hesitated but said, "Sure. I'll watch your dance."

The girls stopped the music several times and argued about how to do certain moves. Olivia tried to be open-minded and said, "I'm not sure who is right. Why don't we do it Maracelli's way until we can ask at class on Thursday?"

After they ran through the dance one whole time without stopping, Shayla suggested that they do each other's makeup. "We can practice for the recital," she said.

April interrupted and said, "That was cool watching your dance but maybe we can do something outside now."

Olivia was having fun dancing and she loved the idea of playing around with makeup, but knew it was time to listen to April's suggestions of what to do. "I think April's right. It's so nice outside. We can play out there until my mom calls us in for dinner," she said in support of April.

The girls took turns on the tire swing in the back yard and played tag until they couldn't run anymore. They fell down on the grass and April suggested that they find different animal shapes in the clouds.

After they got up, Olivia commented, "I have never looked for things in the clouds before. That was so cool! I'm glad that we listened to you, April. It was a great idea to come outside to play instead of staying in the house all day."

LET'S DISCUSS

1   When the girls were arguing about dance moves, what did Olivia do to show she was an open-minded leader?

2   How did Olivia include April and show that she was open-minded to her ideas?

3   What may have happened if the girls hadn't listened to April and just stayed inside the whole playdate?

4   Why is it important to be an open-minded leader?

5   In what ways could you demonstrate that you are an open-minded leader?

LEADERSHIP LEARNING ACTIVITY

In the upper box on the next page, draw a picture of a person or group of people being closed-minded and ignoring someone. In the lower box, change your picture of the person or group to show people now being open-minded and inclusive of that same person.

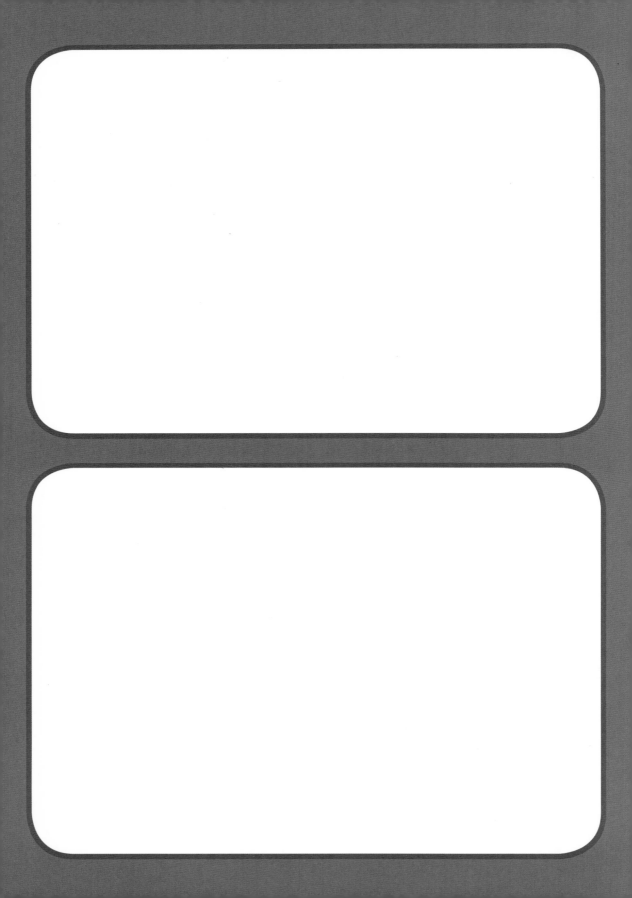

PABLO
THE PATIENT LEADER

*"Patience is waiting with
a happy heart."*

UNKNOWN AUTHOR

DEFINITION

Patient Leader – You are able to wait calmly.

WHAT IT MEANS FOR YOU

When you are a patient leader, you are able to calmly and quietly wait your turn. If someone is busy or already talking to someone else, you quietly wait your turn to speak with them. You demonstrate patience by waiting calmly in line, raising your hand in class, and not interrupting others when they are speaking.

PABLO
THE PATIENT LEADER

The ride to the aquarium seemed to take forever. "I can't wait to get off this bus," said Tad Greene.

Pablo smiled at his friend and said, "We're almost there. I heard the aquarium has a cool underwater tunnel where sharks swim over our heads, and there is a stingray exhibit where we can actually pet the stingrays. This is going to be the best field trip ever."

When the bus finally pulled up to the aquarium, the kids all stood up and tried to push their way to the front. Pablo couldn't wait to get off the bus either but he stood at his seat and waited his turn to start moving forward.

"Come on, Pablo!" shouted Tad.

Their teacher, Mr. Beardsly, waited for everyone to join him at the entrance to the aquarium. With a stern look and a serious, deep voice, he gave the following directions for the day: "This is not a free for all today. Each class will be with their homeroom teacher and two other chaperones. We are all wearing the same orange t-shirts and should be easy to spot. I want you to stay with your group and not wander off. If you need to use the restroom, please make sure a chaperone escorts you. Also, there will be no pushing, running, or jumping in front of others in line. Raise your hand to answer questions. And, most importantly, treat the staff and the animals with respect. We will be leaving promptly at 2:00pm so I want you to start lining up in the atrium by 1:45pm. That means if you are planning on going to the gift shop, you need to make your purchases and get back here on time!"

Pablo's group went through the underwater tunnel first. "There's a hammerhead shark!" Tad excitedly pointed out to Pablo.

The guide told them all about the different types of fish and sea creatures at the aquarium. "How many different species do you think we have here at the aquarium?" she asked.

Kids were all yelling out different answers.

She pointed to Pablo, who had his hand raised. "Thank you for raising your hand. What do you think, young man?"

Pablo answered, "100."

She smiled and said, "Good guess, but we actually have over 1,000 different species throughout the aquarium. I won't be able to tell you about all of them but I'll share information about a good number of some of the more interesting ones.

When the group arrived at the stingray exhibit, the guide said, "Anyone who wants a turn petting a stingray, please form a line around the edge of the tank. Please be gentle when you reach in and use only two fingers when touching them." Again, everyone starting pushing their way to the front.

"Please don't push, everyone will get a chance," she reminded them. Pablo waited patiently until it was his turn. The guide then asked if anyone would like to put on a pair of chest-high water-proof waders and join the scientist in the tank.

Most of the kids started jumping up and down and yelling, "Pick me! Pick me!"

Pablo shot his arm up in the air but didn't yell out or jump up and down. The guide had noticed his good behavior all day and happily picked Pablo to go in the tank.

Pablo couldn't believe how awesome the experience was. He thought that being in the tank and petting the stingrays was the coolest thing he had ever done in his whole life.

At the gift shop, Pablo waited patiently in line to make his purchase. He couldn't wait to show his family the rubber stingray he bought and tell them all about his special day.

LET'S DISCUSS

1. What are a few of the ways Pablo showed he was a patient leader?

2. Why do you think the guide happily picked Pablo to go in the stingray tank?

3. How do you think it made the guide feel when most of the kids were pushing and yelling out?

4. Why is it important to be patient?

5. In what ways could you demonstrate that you are a patient leader?

LEADERSHIP LEARNING ACTIVITY

List six different ways that you can show you are a patient leader. Think of different environments in which you can demonstrate patience (e.g. at home, school, clubs, sports, shopping).

1 _____
_____
_____

2 _____
_____
_____

3 _____
_____
_____

4 _____
_____
_____

5 _____
_____
_____

6 _____
_____
_____

QUINN
THE QUIET LEADER

"Silence is Golden."

ANCIENT PROVERB

DEFINITION

Quiet Leader – You are calm and silent when necessary.

WHAT IT MEANS FOR YOU

When you are a quiet leader, you are able to be calm and silent when necessary. You can sit still and are comfortable in complete silence. You focus on what others say and are able to give your undivided attention. Because you are a quiet leader, you often hear things that other people miss.

QUINN
THE QUIET LEADER

During art class, Quinn listened intently to Ms. Samuelsson describe what she was looking for in the nature photography project. "I want you to take a picture of any type of nature setting or of some kind of wildlife using a phone or camera. I want your photograph to represent who you are in some way. For example, are you energetic and act like the squirrels running around the park? Are you colorful like a rainbow? Do you feel at peace watching the ocean waves? The possibilities are limitless. The only rule is that you have to be the one taking the picture. Does anyone have any questions?" she asked.

As they brainstormed over lunch, Gabby Herrera asked Quinn, "What do you want to take a picture of for the nature project? What about kids on the playground? What about my dog, Chester? I know. How about the turtles on Black River Pond?"

"Did I ever tell you that I think your parents named you very appropriately?" Quinn said with a smile.

"What's that supposed to mean?" asked Gabby. "You know very well that my real named is Gabriella," she said with her arms crossed.

"Yes, but didn't they start calling you Gabby around the same time that you started talking?" Quinn asked jokingly.

"Very funny. My mother says that I'm enthusiastic," Gabby said proudly.

"That you are. Now let's think about this nature photography project for art class," suggested Quinn.

Since they had a week until the project was due, the girls decided to ask Gabby's parents take them to the Hansen Bird Preserve the following weekend.

As soon as they arrived at the visitor's center, Gabby excitedly said, "I'm going to have my mom take my picture by the Preserve sign for my project and I'll be done!"

Quinn quickly reminded Gabby, "Ms. Samuelsson said that you have to take the picture. You can't be in the picture unless you are holding the phone and taking a selfie."

"Oh. I missed that part," Gabby said quietly.

As the girls walked up to an observation platform by one of the ponds, Gabby chatted non-stop about everything. Quinn smiled at her friend and said, "Did you know that the words silent and listen are spelled with the same letters?"

Gabby thought about it a minute and said, "Oh, sorry. I guess I was talking a lot again."

Quinn elbowed her friend and pointed to the pond. "You should take a picture of the noisy, quacking ducks," she teased.

"Great idea!" Gabby said. "I know I should be upset that you think I am like a quacking duck. But it just so happens that I like ducks!" she said with a big smile as she took a picture of them.

Quinn then asked Mr. and Mrs. Herrera if she could go to the observation deck overlooking the mountain ridge. "It's within sight of the Preserve's cafeteria if you want to grab lunch while I figure out what I'm going to take a picture of," she suggested.

As she sat quietly for several minutes, she heard a soft flapping sound above her. It was a beautiful, graceful eagle. She watched it fly for several more minutes and then it landed on a branch about 30 feet away from her. She quietly lifted her mom's camera from its case and zeroed in on the eagle and took a few pictures.

When she turned in her project to Ms. Samuelsson the next week, the teacher was amazed at her picture. She said to Quinn, "You must have been incredibly quiet and still to get a picture this close to an eagle. You always lead with such quiet grace, I can see why you chose to take a picture of a powerful but quiet bird. Great job!"

LET'S DISCUSS

1. What did Quinn do to be a quiet leader in Ms. Samuelsson's class?

2. Why do you think Gabby missed Ms. Samuelsson's directions about who was supposed to take the picture?

3. Why do you think Quinn was able to take a picture of the eagle?

4. Why is it important sometimes to be a quiet leader?

5. In what ways could you demonstrate that you are a quiet leader?

LEADERSHIP LEARNING ACTIVITY

Look at the number line and circle where you think you fall on the scale as a quiet leader (0 – Noisy Quacking Duck to 10 – Silent Eagle)?

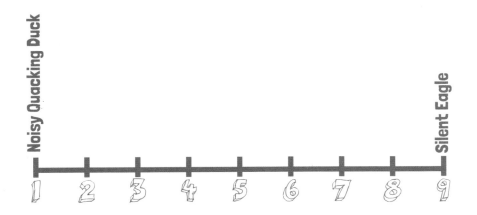

If you selected somewhere from 2 to 8, what would you call your leader level (Quiet Quail, Chirping Cockatoo, etc.)? Be creative and have fun naming your personal leader level.

_____

Based on your response above, circle any of the following that you can improve upon to develop into a more effective quiet leader:

Talk less

Listen more

Focus on what others say

Sit quietly

Be patient and calm

Give your undivided attention

RILEY
THE RESPECTFUL LEADER

"Respect for ourselves guides our morals, respect for others guides our manners."

LAURENCE STERN

DEFINITION

Respectful Leader – You are considerate of others.

WHAT IT MEANS FOR YOU

When you are a respectful leader, you are courteous and polite to others. You are well-behaved and use good manners in your interactions with others. You are responsible with belongings and get along with peers, family members, and those in authority.

RILEY
THE RESPECTFUL LEADER

Riley smiled at the lunch lady and said, "May I please have mashed potatoes with my turkey?" As she walked away she made sure to say, "Thank you, Ms. Kathy. Have a great day."

"Why do you always tell the lunch ladies to have a great day?" her friend, Jenna Barto, asked.

"I don't know. I guess because my mom says we should always use good manners. Why don't you say something to them?"

"Because we're always in a hurry and it would slow up the line if we all stopped and chatted with the lunch ladies every day like you do," Jenna teased.

"Really, Jenna! The world would be a much happier place if everyone took a second to say please and thank you," Riley urged her friend. "Anyway, do you want to go to the movies with me, Colleen, and Winnie tomorrow night?" she asked.

"I'll ask my parents. My two dumb older brothers probably have a game tomorrow night and they'll want to drag me along like usual," Jenna responded.

"You shouldn't call your brothers dumb. I wish I had a sibling. You're so lucky to have three brothers!" Riley told her.

"Well, at least you don't get made fun of all the time and get put inside a garbage can after every holiday meal!" exclaimed Jenna.

"That's a point!" Riley said with a smile.

After school the next day, Riley was so happy when Jenna called to say she could go to the movies with them. "It's only because she couldn't take my whining anymore," laughed Jenna.

The girls all got dropped off at Riley's house around 6:00pm. "Mom, thanks for being willing to drive us to the movies. Could we please leave a little early so we can get popcorn and drinks?" asked Riley.

Jenna looked surprised and whispered, "Wow. You even use good manners with your own parents. I think my mom would fall over if my brothers or I talked to her like that."

"You should try it," encouraged Riley. "Who knows, maybe you won't even have to whine to get your way next time!"

When Riley's mom dropped her off, Jenna said, "Thanks, Mrs. C.! That sure was better than sitting at my brothers' game all night."

"You should say thank you to your parents for letting you go. But have the phone ready in case they pass out and you have to call 911," teased Riley.

Jenna walked into the kitchen and said, "Hey Mom. Thanks for letting me go to the movies with Riley, Coleen, and Winnie tonight. May I please have a cup of milk and a cookie?"

Although her mom didn't pass out, she did stand there for a few seconds with her mouth hanging open and her eyes as wide as saucers. "Sure, Jenna. With manners like that, you can have the rest of the cookies all to yourself." Jenna thought about Riley and smiled.

LET'S DISCUSS

1   What are a few of the ways Riley demonstrated that she was a respectful leader?

2   Why was Jenna so shocked that Riley used good manners all the time?

3   How do you think it made Jenna's mom feel when Jenna was finally respectful and used good manners?

4   Why is it important to be respectful to others?

5   In what ways could you demonstrate that you are a respectful leader?

LEADERSHIP LEARNING ACTIVITY

Read the following conversation bubbles on the left and respond as a respectful leader with manners in the conversation bubbles on the right.

SHAWN
THE SERVANT LEADER

"True leadership is servanthood.
Put the interests of others at
the center of your decisions."

UNKNOWN AUTHOR

DEFINITION

Servant Leader – You unselfishly help others to be successful.

WHAT IT MEANS FOR YOU

When you are a servant leader, you unselfishly focus on other people's needs and help them to be successful at that which they are trying to accomplish. You help individuals to do their best without expecting anything in return. For example, you may teach someone how to improve a skill, let someone go before you in line, or help do someone else's chores without expecting anything from them.

SHAWN
THE SERVANT LEADER

Shawn was working on his kickflip when Bo Mosser and Flick Foust arrived at the skatepark. "Good one!" Bo said to his friend. "If I perfect my switch ollie today and we feel good about all of our tricks, I think we should make the video tomorrow for the online coolest skateboarding video competition. We only have a few days left," he suggested.

"You're right," Shawn agreed. "Man, I think we have a great chance at winning!" he continued. Shawn, Bo, and Flick had been skateboarding together for over three years and were really excited to showcase their latest tricks for the video documentary. The winners of the competition would get the chance to meet with two local legendary skateboarding professionals and learn some of their tricks.

"Hey, there's Evan Branch," Flick said as he tossed his head in Evan's direction.

"Why does he even bother skating on a board like that?" remarked Flick. Flick and Bo quickly skated away, their long hair flying behind them on the ramp.

Shawn stayed back to say hi to Evan. "What's up? Have you entered your video for the competition yet?

"Nah. The deck of my skateboard's cracked and my axels are trashed. My stepdad won't get me a new board and I can't even try any of the cool tricks you guys are working on," Evan said disappointedly.

Shawn felt bad for Evan. Evan was a year younger than him, and he seemed to always be skating alone. Evan had potential as a skateboarder. He had great balance and good basic skills. "He just needs some good coaching and a better board," Shawn thought. Although Shawn needed to be working on his own moves, he said to Evan, "Hey man, why don't you try some tricks on my board and I'll give you some pointers if you need any?"

Bo and Flick soon came over to Shawn and exclaimed, "Dude, what are you doing? We need to get ready for tomorrow!"

"I will be! I'm letting Evan get used to my board because I'm going to let him use it and help him make his video for the competition after we're done with ours," Shawn replied.

"Why would you do that?" Flick asked.

"What if his video turns out better than ours?" said Bo.

"It's no big deal," said Shawn. "I'm just helping him out a little. Our video is going to be awesome!"

A few weeks later, the results of the competition were posted online. Neither of them had won. Shawn was disappointed but it didn't really matter that much. He skated because he loved it, not because he needed to prove he was better than anyone else. He also started working with Evan any time he saw him at the skatepark. He felt great that Evan was improving and starting to land some of the tricks that he was working on with him. He was glad to have another diehard skater in the community.

LET'S DISCUSS

1. What did Shawn do to be a servant leader to Evan?

2. How might Shawn have positively influenced his friends?

3. How do you think it made Evan feel to have Shawn unselfishly help him?

4. Why would anyone want to unselfishly help others?

5. In what ways could you demonstrate that you are a servant leader?

LEADERSHIP LEARNING ACTIVITY

Fill out the two coupons for two different people or groups that you want to help. Consider doing something nice for a family member, a friend, or a neighbor, or volunteering for a good cause. Write to whom the coupon is for and how you plan on helping.

COUPON FOR SERVICE

To: _____

For:

_____

_____

_____

COUPON FOR SERVICE

To: _____

For:

_____

_____

_____

TYSON
THE TRUSTWORTHY LEADER

"Be true to your work, your word, and your friend."

HENRY DAVID THOREAU

DEFINITION
Trustworthy Leader – You do what you say you are going to do.

WHAT IT MEANS FOR YOU
When you are a trustworthy leader, you demonstrate through your words and actions that others can trust you. Other people know that you will follow through on your promises and honor your commitments. You don't make promises that you can't keep. You do the right thing even when others don't.

TYSON
THE TRUSTWORTHY LEADER

"Tyson, don't forget that you and your sister promised to help out on Pop Pop and Nana's farm this Saturday," his mom reminded him.

"I know, mom. Celeste and I talked about it this morning before school. We'll ride our bikes over there first thing on Saturday morning so we can milk the cows and do the other chores for Pop Pop."

On Saturday morning, Tyson and Celeste left the house before their parents were even out of bed. When they had finished milking the cows and feeding the chickens, they came into their grandparents' old farmhouse and gave them each a huge hug. "How are you feeling since your surgery, Pop Pop?" asked Tyson.

"You're not riding wheelies around Nana in that wheelchair, are you?" teased Celeste.

"I'll be back to working this farm sooner than those doctors say I will," said Pop Pop. "I'm sure you kids would rather be playing with your friends than wrestling roosters."

"We like coming here," Tyson said with a smile. "We're happy to help. So what else needs to be done?"

Pop Pop explained the rest of the chores and reminded them about the old bull in the pasture. "Old Billy will leave you alone but he does like to wander off if the gate isn't latched properly. He's a stubborn old fella to bring back in. You'll remember to latch it tight if you go out to the pond, won't you?" he asked.

"Of course," Tyson agreed.

When they had finished all the chores, they ran back to the shed to get their fishing poles. They were so excited to get to the pond to see if they could catch the giant catfish that they forgot to latch the gate tightly. Tyson was getting ready to cast when he remembered Pop Pop's warning. "The gate!" he yelled back to Celeste as he ran for the fence. Old Billy was rubbing up against the gate and just about ready to break loose when Tyson got there. He latched it just in time. "Phew! That could have been a disaster!" he said to himself.

When he got back to the pond, he told Celeste about the close call with Old Billy.

"Thank goodness you kept your promise to Pop Pop," she said. "If Old Billy got loose, Nana definitely wouldn't give us any of her fresh baked chocolate chip cookies!" she teased.

They decided to call it a day and head back in to see their grandparents. They were relieved to find fresh baked chocolate chip cookies and hot cocoa waiting for them when they returned to the old farmhouse.

LET'S DISCUSS

1. What did Tyson do to demonstrate that he was a trustworthy leader?

2. How might Pop Pop have felt if Old Billy had gotten loose?

3. Has anyone ever broken your trust? How did that make you feel?

4. Why is it important to be trustworthy?

5. In what ways could you demonstrate that you are a trustworthy leader?

LEADERSHIP LEARNING ACTIVITY

Answer the following trivia questions about being a trustworthy leader:

Question 1

Which one of the following best describes someone who is trustworthy?

- a) keeps their promise
- b) doesn't show up
- c) lies to cover up mistakes
- d) goes fishing instead

Question 2

As a trustworthy leader, if you make a commitment to do something, you:

- a) leave and let someone else finish what you started
- b) can be counted on to complete the job and do it right
- c) make excuses for why you can't finish the job
- d) run and hide if you can't complete your commitment

Question 3

Which one of the following best describes leaders who are trustworthy?

- a) can always be counted on to follow through on their commitment
- b) are always honest
- c) do not make promises that they can't keep
- d) all of the above

Answers: Question 1: a)   Question 2: b)   Question 3: d)

UMA
THE UNDERSTANDING LEADER

"One of the most beautiful qualities of true friendship is to understand and to be understood."

LUCIUS ANNAEUS SENECA

DEFINITION

Understanding Leader – You respond appropriately to another person's feelings.

WHAT IT MEANS FOR YOU

When you are an understanding leader, you are compassionate and empathize with other people. You can identify your own feelings and respond appropriately to the feelings of others. You take time to show others that you care for them and are willing to be there for them.

UMA
THE UNDERSTANDING LEADER

Uma wondered why her friend, Ashlynn Knight, wasn't in school. She and Melena Parson had just spent the afternoon at Ashlynn's house the day before and she seemed fine. "I hope everything is okay," Uma thought to herself.

The next day, Ashlynn came to school with tears in her eyes and Uma asked her friend, "What's wrong? You look so sad."

"My dog, Tulip, died yesterday before school. I was getting ready to feed her like I always do in the morning and she wouldn't get up from her dog bed. I even tried tossing her favorite squeaky toy at her and she still wouldn't move," Ashlynn said with tears starting to flow down her cheeks.

Uma reached out and gave her friend a big hug and said, "I'm so sorry, Ashlynn. I know how much you loved Tulip." Uma felt very sad for her friend. "Is there anything I can do to make you feel better?" she asked.

"I don't know. I just wish my parents hadn't made me come to school today," Ashlynn said, trying not to cry again.

Throughout the day, Uma thought about what she could do to make Ashlynn feel better. She had an idea.

During art class, Uma asked their teacher, Mr. Webber, if she could do a special art project for Ashlynn to try and cheer her up. At the end of the day, Uma told Ashlynn that she made something special for her and asked if it would be okay to come over after school.

"Of course. That's really sweet of you," Ashlynn said.

Uma's mom dropped her off at Ashlynn's house about an hour later. Uma gave her the special picture that she had drawn of Tulip. She had also included a lot of funny stories and names they had for Tulip, including her favorite story about how Tulip got her name when she was a puppy. They had just brought her home from the doggy rescue and let her loose in the yard and before they could stop her, she ran into her mom's flower bed and pulled out every single tulip her mom had planted.

Ashlynn laughed and cried as she looked at the funny picture and read all the special things Uma wrote. She told Uma, "That was the most caring thing you could have done. I will keep this picture forever and think of the happy times that I had with Tulip every time I look at it. Thanks for cheering me up and being such a kind and understanding friend."

LET'S DISCUSS

1 What did Uma do to demonstrate that she was an understanding leader?

2 How do you think it made Ashlynn feel that her friend tried to be so thoughtful and understanding?

3 Has anyone ever gone out of their way to be supportive and understanding for you? How did that make you feel?

4 Why is it important to be thoughtful and understanding?

5 In what ways could you demonstrate that you are an understanding leader to someone else?

LEADERSHIP LEARNING ACTIVITY

As an understanding leader, write a text message to your friend B who has just found out that her grandmother has died. Use the message to show her that you care.

B

VIVIAN
THE VIRTUOUS LEADER

"All the gold which is under or upon the earth is not enough to give in exchange for virtue."

PLATO

DEFINITION

Virtuous Leader – You choose to do the right thing even when no one is looking.

WHAT IT MEANS FOR YOU

When you are a virtuous leader, you are honest and true to yourself and others. You choose to do the right thing even when no one is looking. You have integrity and are able to look yourself in the mirror and feel good about the person you are and the choices that you make.

VIVIAN
THE VIRTUOUS LEADER

It was Friday night and Vivian and her friends had plans to meet at the bowling alley to grab a slice of pizza and play pool before heading to the movies. Vivian and her closest friend, Maddie Tyler, arrived first as usual. They were shooting a game of pool when Nic Morrison and Skylar Boone finally got there. "You're 20 minutes late again," said Maddie.

"Yeah. Yeah. It takes time to look this good," said Nic with a sly smile.

"No. It's more like Nic's mom was yelling at him and threatening to not let him go tonight because he hadn't straightened up his room like he promised. I had to sit and watch Jeopardy on TV with Granny Melba until he was done. She yells at me every time I try to answer," complained Skylar.

"Should we order just one pizza to share?" interrupted Vivian.

They all agreed so Vivian went to the counter to order their pizza and drinks.

When she was walking back to the pool table, she saw a $20 bill lying on the ground. She looked around and didn't see anyone standing close by so she picked it up. "I wonder who this belongs to?" she thought. She took it to the counter and handed it to the cashier. "I found this by the trash can. I'm sure someone will be looking for it," she said.

Vivian told her friends about the money that she had found and Nic yelled at her, "Why didn't you keep it? You could have paid for the movie or at least bought us all popcorn and candy!"

"It wasn't mine. I wasn't going to keep it," Vivian said defensively.

At the end of the movie, Nic and Skylar were whispering and then said to Vivian and Maddie, "We have an idea. There's a different movie starting right after this in Theatre 3. Let's sneak in and watch that one for free."

Vivian hesitated and said, "I'm sure we could get away with it but I just don't feel right about it. If you guys definitely want to watch that movie, I'll go and buy another ticket."

"Vivian's right," said Maddie. "I don't feel right about not paying. I have enough money to get another ticket if that's what you guys want to do."

Nic paused and said, "That's alright. We can go back to the bowling alley for a little while. I didn't get to show off all of my mad pool skills yet anyway."

LET'S DISCUSS

1 What did Vivian do to demonstrate that she was a virtuous leader?

2 How do you think Vivian's choices affected her friends' decisions?

3 What would you do if you found a $20 bill on the floor?

4 Why is it important to make good choices even when others aren't looking?

5 In what ways could you demonstrate that you are a virtuous leader?

LEADERSHIP LEARNING ACTIVITY

As a virtuous leader, what would you do in the following situations? Respond in the right-hand column.

If...	You would...
Your friend tells you that they found out what all the answers are for tomorrow's math test…	
You are playing cards with your brother and you see all of his cards…	
You find a cool jacket, the kind that you have wanted for a long time, lying on the ground after school…	

WILLOW
THE LEADER WITH THE WINNING ATTITUDE

"It is our attitude at the beginning of a difficult task which, more than anything else, will affect its successful outcome."

WILLIAM JAMES

DEFINITION

Leader with a Winning Attitude – You believe in yourself and others.

WHAT IT MEANS FOR YOU

When you are a leader with a winning attitude, you believe in yourself and others and work hard to achieve your goals. You don't allow obstacles or mistakes to give you a negative attitude. You encourage and build confidence in others and help them celebrate their successes. You are a good sport and know how to be both a good winner and a good loser. You take the time to compliment others, even opponents, when they play well.

WILLOW
THE LEADER WITH THE WINNING ATTITUDE

Willow's volleyball team, the Falcons, were playing their biggest rival, the Bulldogs. Before going out on the court, Coach Jenn tried to encourage the team and said, "Girls, this is a big game but remember that we're just here to play volleyball! Play your best and don't forget to have fun!"

The girls were doing great. Each team won one set and the whole gym was energized going in to the third and final set. The points went back and forth and the Falcons were up 20–17! The Falcon's weakest passer, Sammie Duncan, was beginning to fall apart and the Bulldogs knew it. Sammie repeatedly shanked and the Falcons lost three points in a row. The score was tied at 20–20 when Coach Jenn called a timeout.

Claudia Gainer spoke up before Coach Jenn could say anything. "Sammie should be subbed out! We're going to lose because of her!" Sammie hung her head, embarrassed at how poorly she was playing.

Willow jumped in to defend her teammate. "Sammie doesn't need to be subbed out!" She looked at Sammie and said, "You've been playing great today. You can do this! You've done it a million times before. You just need to get behind the ball and read your server. Remember what Coach Jenn said before the game – we are just here to play volleyball! We all need to play our best and not get hung up on a few mistakes!" Claudia rolled her eyes at Willow.

Coach Jenn smiled at her and said, "Willow's right. Remember that every time the ball moves, there's potential for a point. Either you're going to get the point or the other team will. That's why you can't get down on yourself or your teammates. The moment your attitude changes or takes a different direction, it determines the outcome of the game – good or bad!"

The last minute of the game was intense! Sammie was able to return two tough serves and the girls worked hard to pull off a 25–23 victory over the Bulldogs.

As the girls were shaking hands with the other team, Willow complimented several of the other girls and said to the Bulldog's coach, "You guys played great. Your team was really tough!"

As they were walking back to the locker room, Sammie said to Willow, "Thanks for sticking up for me and helping me get my confidence back."

Willow smiled at her and said, "Anytime. I knew if we worked hard as a team and believed in ourselves, that we could do it!"

LET'S DISCUSS

1. What did Willow do to demonstrate that she was a leader with a winning attitude?

2. How do you think the Bulldog's players and coach felt when Willow complimented them on being a great team and playing hard?

3. Why is it important to believe in yourself and others?

4. Why is it important to be both a good winner and a good loser?

5. What can you do to demonstrate that you are a leader with a winning attitude?

LEADERSHIP LEARNING ACTIVITY

Write a letter to yourself to remind yourself what it will take for you to share a winning attitude with others. Include one specific way that you can demonstrate that you have a winning attitude in the next week.

Dear _____

_____

_____

_____

_____

_____

This week I will demonstrate a winning attitude by: _____

_____

_____

_____

_____

_____

With a winning attitude,

_____

XAVIER
THE LEADER WITH
THE X-FACTOR

> "Why be ordinary when you
> can be extraordinary."

AUTHOR UNKNOWN

DEFINITION

Leader with the X-Factor – Others recognize your unique leadership.

WHAT IT MEANS FOR YOU

When you are a leader with the X-factor, others are drawn to you because you are likeable, happy, confident, and true to yourself and others. You make new friends easily and always look for the good in other people.

XAVIER
THE LEADER WITH THE X-FACTOR

Xavier's family moved to a new house over the weekend and it was he and his younger brother's first day at their new school. "I'm really nervous," Bryson admitted to Xavier.

"I understand," said Xavier. "I'm a little nervous, too. But even more than that, I'm excited for us to make some new friends," he said encouragingly to his little brother.

"Easy for you to say. You make new friends everywhere you go," sighed Bryson. "Why is it so easy for you and so hard for me?" he asked.

"Well, maybe you just need to be more confident in yourself and not act so shy around new people," Xavier suggested. "If you look for good in people, you usually find it. Then you have something that you like about the person already," he said with a smile.

Sure enough, Xavier started making new friends within a few minutes of being on the bus. He introduced himself and said hi to two of the boys in the row across from him. "What's up? My name's Xavier. Anything important I should know about the school or Ms. Lambert, my fifth grade teacher?"

The two other boys introduced themselves and they all started talking immediately. One of the boys, Dominick Lyons, was in Ms. Lambert's homeroom as well and said he would show Xavier to class. Bryson watched in disbelief as his brother was already asking what the boys did after school and if they played any sports. "How does he do it?" wondered Bryson.

Xavier told Dominick that he wanted to walk his younger brother to his fourth grade class before going to their homeroom. Dominick said, "That's fine. It's on the way to our room. I'll show you."

On the way down the hall, Xavier said, "What's up?" "Nice hat," "Cool glasses," to several different people. "He has no fear," thought Bryson.

Bryson smiled shyly as his homeroom teacher introduced him to the class. The teacher sat him next to a tough-looking boy named Pierce Parker. Pierce said hi to Bryson but he just nodded his head and quickly looked away. Bryson started to worry that he wouldn't know how to make new friends. He thought about what Xavier had said to him about being confident and trying to look for good in people. "I guess I can try," he thought to himself. Using Xavier's example, he leaned over to Pierce and said, "Anything I need to know about Mrs. Forney?"

Pierce whispered back, "Yeah. She's meaner than a snake and doesn't like when we talk in class!" Bryson looked scared. Pierce laughed and said, "I'm just kidding. She's a great teacher. We can talk more over lunch."

Bryson thought, "Well I guess I know one of the good things about Pierce. He's a funny kid."

Bryson decided to be a little more open to talking to other new kids, and surprisingly, the rest of the day went better than he had expected. It made him realize how glad he was to have Xavier as his brother.

LET'S DISCUSS

1   Why were other kids so drawn to Xavier?

2   Why do you think Xavier had an easier time making friends than Bryson?

3   Why is it important to look for good in other people?

4   Why is it sometimes hard meeting new people?

5   What can you do to demonstrate that you are a leader with the X-factor?

LEADERSHIP LEARNING ACTIVITY

Circle the following X-factors that you possess. You can select more than one. If you think of other traits that make you special, add them at the end of the list.

Confident   Talented   Happy

Mannerly   Caring   Complimentary to Others

Helpful   Reliable   Friendly

Nice   Generous   Smart

Careful   Assertive   Approachable

Others: _____

YIN
THE YIELDING LEADER

> "All men make mistakes, but
> a good man yields when he
> knows his course is wrong."

SOPHOCLES

DEFINITION

Yielding Leader – You are willing to admit when you are wrong.

WHAT IT MEANS FOR YOU

When you are a yielding leader, you are willing to admit if you made a mistake or were in the wrong. You don't let your pride prevent you from admitting to someone else that they are right and you are wrong. If you do get in an argument, you focus on what you could do differently, not on what the other person should do differently. You are also willing to be teachable and correctable.

YIN
THE YIELDING LEADER

Yin and his twin brother, Ping, enjoyed playing all different kinds of games together. They were particularly competitive when they played chess and a game called Settlers of Catan.

The boys set up the chess board but disagreed about who was white and who was black in the last game. "I know I went first last night which means I was white," Ping argued. Their father walked into the room and Ping asked him, "You watched our chess game last night, didn't you? Do you remember who was white and who was black?"

His father thought for a moment and said, "Ping, I believe you were white." Ping looked at Yin and crossed his arms with a smirk on his face.

Yin looked at his brother and said, "You must be right then. I was wrong. I will be white tonight."

After their game of chess, their father asked if the boys wanted to play a game of Settlers of Catan. "Sure. I'll win that tonight as well," Yin teased.

After an hour, the boys were tied at 9–9 and their father had 7 points. The boys' competitive spirits were in full motion again. It was Ping's turn and as he was taking a long time deciding what to do, Yin excitedly grabbed the dice and rolled a seven which meant that Ping had to lose half his cards. "I can build! That's 10 points! I win!" Yin said.

Ping was upset. He said he could've done something for the win and Yin didn't have the right to take the dice and go so quickly.

Their father asked Ping, "Could you have scored, son?"

"I would have bought a development card and if that was a victory point, I would have won," Ping responded. Their father flipped over the next card and sure enough it was a victory point.

Painfully Yin gave Ping the win. He was about ready to argue that Ping took too long and that he should have made the decision to buy a card sooner, but instead he said, "Good game, Ping. I was wrong and shouldn't have taken the dice from you. It was a good win. Now who wants to play again?"

LET'S DISCUSS

1 What did Yin do at the beginning of the chess game to demonstrate that he was a yielding leader?

2 What did Yin say at the end of the Settlers of Catan game to show that he was a yielding leader?

3 Why is it respectful to another person to admit when you are wrong and they are right?

4 After a disagreement, why is it important to focus on what you could have done differently rather than on what the other person should have done differently?

5 What can you do to demonstrate that you are a yielding leader?

LEADERSHIP LEARNING ACTIVITY

Unscramble the following phrase and then answer the question below.

MITAD HNEW OYU RAE RWNOG

_ _ _ _ _   _ _ _ _   _ _ _   _ _ _   _ _ _ _ _

Share an example of when you have admitted to making a mistake:

_____

_____

_____

_____

_____

_____

_____

ZACHARY
THE ZEALOUS LEADER

"Live your life as an exclamation
rather than an explanation."

SIR ISAAC NEWTON

DEFINITION

Zealous Leader – You are filled with excitement and enthusiasm.

WHAT IT MEANS FOR YOU

When you are a zealous leader, you are filled with excitement and enthusiasm. You are inspired or passionate about a cause. You spend a lot of time or energy in supporting something that you strongly believe in. You are eager to take on duties and responsibilities that make a difference.

ZACHARY THE ZEALOUS LEADER

Zachary was running for student council president. He decided to run as soon as elections opened up a few weeks ago. He had been on the student council for the last three years, but now that he was a fifth grader, he was finally able to run for president!

"I can't believe election day is finally here!" Zachary said to his friend and campaign manager, Ellis Geoffries. "I can't wait to give my speech and share some of the great ideas we've come up with," he said excitedly.

"Well, I'm glad you can't wait because you're up next," said Ellis.

During his speech, Zachary's passion showed clearly as he talked about ideas for food drives and fundraisers in support of community causes, examples of schoolwide celebrations, and other ways to build school pride. He ended his speech by saying, "I strongly believe the student council can lead the way to positive change! I promise, as your leader, to work hard to fulfill my responsibilities and make this the best elementary school around!" He received loud applause and cheers as he sat down.

At the end of the assembly, each student dropped off their votes in the designated ballot boxes. The votes would be counted and the officers and class representatives would be announced at the end of the day.

Zachary stayed positive all day. He knew he had a position on the council even if he didn't win. Regardless of the election outcome, he was honored to serve on the council and lead with academic integrity and exemplary behavior. "Although, I sure am ready to take on additional duties and responsibilities that will make a difference in our school," he said to himself.

Mr. Murphy, the school principal, got on the intercom and began announcing the results of the election. The last position to be announced was that of the student council president. There was a long pause, and then Mr. Murphy congratulated Zachary on winning.

On the way out of school, Mr. Murphy stopped Zachary and said, "I look forward to you leading the council with as much enthusiasm and passion as you showed earlier during your speech. Job well done. Congratulations on being council president."

LET'S DISCUSS

1. What types of things did Zachary do to be a zealous leader?

2. Why do you think Zachary was elected as student council president?

3. Why is it important to lead with zeal, excitement, and passion?

4. What kind of things make you excited and zealous?

5. What can you do to demonstrate that you are a zealous leader?

LEADERSHIP LEARNING ACTIVITY

In Question 4, you shared some things that make you excited and zealous. Draw a picture of one of those things.

SUMMARY LEADERSHIP LEARNING ACTIVITY 1

Fill in the blanks below. Try it by memory and
do not to look back for your first attempt.

Alex the _____ Leader

Brooke the _____ Leader

Chloe the _____ - _____ Leader

David the _____ Leader

Enzo the _____ Leader

Fiona the _____ Leader

Gabe the _____ Leader

Hunter the _____ Leader

Kevin the _____ Leader

Lilly the _____ Leader

Matt the _____ - _____ Leader

Natalie the _____ Leader

Olivia the _____-_____Leader

Pablo the _____ Leader

Quinn the _____ Leader

Riley the _____ Leader

Shawn the _____ Leader

Tyson the _____ Leader

Uma the _____ Leader

Vivian the _____ Leader

Willow the Leader with the _____

_____

Xavier the Leader with the _____-_____

Yin the _____ Leader

Zachary the _____ Leader

SUMMARY LEADERSHIP LEARNING ACTIVITY 2

Find the following leadership traits in the word search on the next page.

accepting	just	servant
brave	kind	trustworthy
culturallysensitive	listening	understanding
dependable	missionminded	virtuous
encouraging	navigating	winningattitude
fair	openminded	xfactor
grateful	patient	yielding
honest	quiet	zealous
innovative	respectful	

```
L J E N C O U R A G I N G P A X G Z C T M N
L H U S I I J A A N G H O C I F K O U S D K
B H N S M Y T I Y Y A Y K T M A D M L E L P
L H J Y T G N I T P E C C A H I G I T N L G
N G N I T A G I V A N A U P R R L S U O T I
V T F E L B A D N E P E D Q M O U S R H D N
K I N D K Q N J U N E H E K J S F I A Q D W
I X K B V V R H Y S D X V A Y M E O L X W B
T L A N V M O R X U U F A P T T T N L X D U
R D H G Q U T V C O T F R I E N A M Y O I W
U V B A F N C R Y U I N B N I D R I S R X X
S G P H X D A D N T T S G N U L G N E F F I
T A A J Z E F G Z R T E R O Q X W D N A O W
W D T H G R X O K I A R E V K D R E S W P M
O S I O N S Y G Y V G V S A O A L D I L E I
R U E R I T B N S P N A P T F K V S T Y N R
T O N A N A O I Z I I N E I Z F O S I P M Q
H L T M E N F D X X N T C V V L J B V Y I Q
Y A A E T D M L V Y N E T E W K H Y E V N X
X E R F S I X E P B I P F K K P I D F E D F
R Z M H I N U I E U W L U B U X V B L H E V
B Y M K L G D Y I Q E Z L J M T E B I E D I
```

SUMMARY LEADERSHIP LEARNING ACTIVITY 3

Use the clue to name the leadership trait
and write it in the box to the right.

Clue	Trait
You are not afraid to make a personal sacrifice for others	
You unselfishly help others to be successful	
You are filled with excitement and enthusiasm	
You are calm and silent when necessary	
You respond appropriately to another person's feelings	

You pay attention to what others say	
You appreciate the cultural differences in others	
You show fairness and equality to others	
You come up with new ideas	
You stay focused on the task at hand	
You are thankful to others and show them that you appreciate them	
You are open and tolerant, and accept others for who they are	
You are willing to listen to other people's ideas	

You are considerate of others	
You do what you say you are going to do	
You believe in yourself and others	
You use kind words to give others courage, hope, or confidence	
You always tell the truth	
You are able to wait calmly	
Others recognize your unique leadership	
You understand and follow rules, and apply them equally to everyone	

You choose to do the right thing even when no one is looking	
You are willing to admit when you are wrong	
You put a plan in place to achieve your goals	
Others can count on you to do what you say you are going to do	
You are caring and compassionate to others	

SUMMARY LEADERSHIP LEARNING ACTIVITY 4

Who is your favorite leader from all 26 chapters?

_____

What is it about that leader that you like the most?

_____

_____

_____

_____

What are you going to do to be more like that leader?

_____

_____

_____

_____

_____